the lazy girl's
guide to delicious dinners

60 No-Stress, Limited-Mess, Sure-to-Impress Meals

sophia kaur
Creator of A Quick Spoonful

PAGE STREET
PUBLISHING CO.

To My Mom

For as long as I can remember, my first memories have been with my mom. The way she used to hold me and hug me and make sure I knew that the world was mine to conquer. My mother has always given me the strength and love to dream the biggest dreams and then achieve them.

For all those days you would come home after working the whole day and then make a full dinner from scratch, just know that I was always watching. Always hoping that one day I could do this for my family. Even when, as a teenager, I would sit on the kitchen counter and talk to you about my day as you cooked and moved my head to get to the spices. My true love for cooking and food began with watching you.

Thank you for always being the constant in my life. Thank you for teaching me everything I know. Thank you for always believing in me. Thank you for always being in my corner. Thank you for teaching me what it means to be the best mother to my children. Thank you for taking your lunch breaks at work to pick me up from school. Thank you for never once hiring a babysitter. Thank you for never yelling at me, even when I was annoying. Thank you for making the best lunches for school. Thank you for teaching me what being loved means. Thank you for being you.

I can't write enough on this one page to show you what you mean to me, but I know that this book is for you.

I love you.

contents

introduction

Well, hello there! My name is Sophia, I run a social media channel on Instagram and TikTok called @aquickspoonful, and I am a certified lazy girl. Now, hear me out. Being lazy isn't always a bad thing. I am a mom of three and I don't always have a lot of time, so to me, being lazy in the kitchen just means I want to make the best use of my time and am constantly finding ways to get the most bang for my buck. Over the years I have perfected the art of doing more with less, and I am here to lead the revolution for all the lazy girls out there.

Cooking isn't hard if you know the little kitchen hacks to make life easier. I've used my easy cooking tips and approachable recipes to teach my followers how to cook with confidence. As well as my kids and my husband—who couldn't even boil water. I'm not joking . . . he literally ruined one of my pots and I had to throw it away. Now my whole family (and extended social media family) is cooking with ease—and I can help you too.

If you're a busy person, or someone who's just learning how to cook, let this book be your guide. I will show you how to become the master of your kitchen without spending your whole day in it. You'll be making standout dishes that look and taste like they took all day, but only you will know they were a cinch.

Disclaimer: These recipes are so easy and delicious that when you make them for your friends and family, they will ask for more. Often. Again and again.

So, if you're ready to learn how to make amazing recipes the lazy way, let's get to it!

when . . .
you want to
use the fewest
ingredients

I love the simplicity of some meals. It's not that there's so much to do; it's just that a few things put together and cooked the right way can make such a delicious and filling dinner. I find that these meals are usually what I turn to when I want comfort. The meals that make you feel warm and fuzzy inside, the meals that bring back good memories. Welcome to my happy place.

buffalo chicken quesadillas

Imagine if a grilled cheese sandwich and buffalo chicken wings had a baby. This is that baby. This cheesy goodness is a go-to for after-school snacks as well as a full-blown dinner. I will be honest with you: Sometimes I have all the ingredients for this recipe but I don't have the tortillas, so I have made the same thing with thin bread—and sometimes it's better that way.

Makes 4–6 Servings

16 oz (464 g) cream cheese, softened

2 cups (140 g) shredded rotisserie chicken

1 cup (240 ml) buffalo sauce

1 cup (240 ml) ranch dressing

2 cups (226 g) shredded Mexican cheese

2 cups (226 g) shredded mozzarella cheese

10 large flour tortillas

5 tbsp (70 g) butter, divided

In a mixing bowl, combine the softened cream cheese, shredded rotisserie chicken, buffalo sauce, ranch dressing, shredded Mexican cheese and mozzarella cheese. Top a tortilla with this mixture and top the mixture with another tortilla, making a quesadilla. Prep all the tortillas with the mixture and set aside.

In a skillet over medium heat, melt ½ tablespoon (7 g) of butter and place one quesadilla over the melted butter. Toast for about a minute and lift the quesadilla out of the pan, adding another ½ tablespoon (7 g) of butter to the pan before flipping to the other side. Toast for another minute and remove from the pan, then repeat with the remaining quesadillas. Cut into quarters and serve hot.

chicken tetrazzini

Many many moons ago, before memes were a thing, there was a clip from the Dr. Phil show in which a person would just scream, "Chicken Tetrazzini!" and to this day I still scream it that way every time I make this dish. The funny part is I have been making this bake since I first saw that clip. I love Chicken Tetrazzini; the first time I ever had it was as a frozen dinner in college and I was like, "Where has this been all my life?" For me, it's the breadcrumbs that make this meal phenomenal.

Makes 4–6 Servings

1 lb (454 g) spaghetti

10 oz (283 g) condensed cream of chicken soup

10 oz (283 g) condensed cream of mushroom soup

2 cups (480 ml) sour cream

½ cup (120 ml) melted butter

½ cup (120 ml) chicken broth

1 tsp salt

½ tsp pepper

½ tsp garlic powder

½ tsp paprika

1½ cups (170 g) shredded mozzarella cheese

½ cup (57 g) shredded cheddar cheese

½ cup (67 g) frozen peas

1 rotisserie chicken, shredded

½ cup (54 g) Italian breadcrumbs

Preheat the oven to 350°F (176°C).

Cook spaghetti al dente according to package directions. Drain and set aside.

In a bowl, mix together the condensed cream of chicken soup, condensed cream of mushroom soup, sour cream, melted butter, chicken broth, salt, pepper, garlic powder, paprika, mozzarella cheese and cheddar cheese until smooth. Fold in the frozen peas, shredded chicken and cooked spaghetti. Make sure all the pasta is coated and set aside.

Into a 3-quart (2.8-L) oven-safe baking dish, spray nonstick cooking spray and add the noodle mixture. Cover the dish with foil and place it in the oven for 30 minutes. After 30 minutes, take it out of the oven and add the Italian breadcrumbs on top. Bake for another 10 minutes uncovered or until the breadcrumbs are toasty and browned.

Remove the tetrazzini from the oven and let it stand for at least 15 minutes before serving. You're going to need some garlic bread also—you know, as a utensil.

sesame peanut noodles

These noodles are truly ready in 10 minutes. Yes, legitimately 10 minutes. You don't even need to turn the stove on for this, and no it's not a cold pasta. The best part is that this recipe makes so much. I like to keep these noodles in the fridge and would even eat them cold at 1 in the morning when I was writing this book. I am currently eating these noodles while I am writing this recipe! It's a full noodle circle. Also, chewy rice noodles, in my opinion, are the absolute best noodles to eat. I used to have to go to an Asian market to get them, but now every local grocer has these noodles in stock in the international aisle.

Makes 4–6 Servings

1 (9-oz [255-g]) box of Pad Thai rice noodles

Boiling water to cover the noodles

½ cup (129 g) creamy peanut butter

½ cup (120 ml) water

¼ cup (60 ml) soy sauce

½ tsp chili oil

¼ tsp fish sauce

3 tbsp (27 g) brown sugar, unpacked

Juice of 1 lime

2 tsp (10 ml) sesame oil

1 tbsp (8 g) grated garlic

1 tbsp (11 g) black sesame seeds

¼ cup (12 g) chopped green onions

In a bowl, cover the dry Pad Thai rice noodles with boiling water. Let the noodles sit for 5 minutes or until cooked. Leave in the water until ready to toss with the sauce.

In a large bowl, mix the peanut butter, water, soy sauce, chili oil, fish sauce, brown sugar, lime juice, sesame oil and garlic until smooth.

Add the noodles to the sauce and toss well so that all the noodles are coated. If you would like a thinner sauce, add a bit of the cooking water from the noodles.

Transfer the noodles to a serving dish and garnish with sesame seeds and chopped green onions.

shredded italian grinder

This is not your normal sandwich. All the ingredients are finely chopped and come together so much better than when you just stack them on sliced bread. This sandwich went viral on TikTok and for good reason. Most people do add tomato to the mix (I am not a fan so I don't put it in my recipe, but you can definitely add it to yours).

Makes 4–6 Servings

½ lb (226 g) sliced pepperoni

½ lb (226 g) sliced salami

½ lb (226 g) sliced turkey

½ lb (226 g) provolone cheese

⅓ cup (40 g) banana peppers

½ head lettuce

1 tsp oregano

½ red onion

½ cup (120 ml) mayo

1 tsp garlic powder

1 tsp salt

1 tsp pepper

1 tbsp (15 ml) red wine vinegar

4–6 hoagie rolls

Butter, room temperature, for spreading on the rolls

On your cutting board, stack the pepperoni, salami, turkey, provolone cheese, banana peppers, lettuce, oregano and onion. Chop all of these ingredients together until they are finely chopped. I mean super fine.

Place the chopped ingredients in a bowl and add the mayo, garlic powder, salt, pepper and red wine vinegar. Mix well.

Split each hoagie roll in half lengthwise, leaving the two sides of the roll attached. Scoop out some of the bread from each side. Spread the butter on the bread and broil it on low for 1 to 2 minutes, or until golden. Remove from the oven and scoop the filling mixture into each roll. Fold over and enjoy the best sandwiches you've ever had.

orzo meatball soup

Frozen meatballs may be the one staple that is forever in my home. I used to make my own meatballs and store them in the freezer—but then I had three kids. Now I get delicious organic meatballs in the freezer section and my job is so much easier. If you want to make fresh meatballs, or use frozen ones that you've made, you do you, boo. This soup is hearty and filling. It reminds me of Italian wedding soup but has more of a tomato-y base. You can add a bigger pasta if you like, but I love the little tiny orzo in each spoonful. Again—you do you.

Makes 4–6 Servings

2 tbsp (30 ml) olive oil

½ yellow onion, chopped

4–6 cloves garlic, chopped

1 (28-oz [784-g]) can fire roasted tomatoes

4 cups (960 ml) beef broth

1 red bell pepper, chopped

¼ tsp Italian seasoning

½ tsp red pepper flakes

1 tbsp (18 g) salt

1 tbsp (6 g) pepper

1 lb (454 g) frozen meatballs

2 cups (454 g) orzo pasta

¼ cup (6 g) fresh chopped basil

In a pot over medium heat, add the olive oil and onions and sauté until translucent. Add the chopped garlic and heat for another minute. Add in the tomatoes, beef broth, red bell pepper, Italian seasoning, red pepper flakes, salt, pepper and frozen meatballs. Turn the heat to high and bring everything to a boil.

Once the soup is boiling, add the orzo pasta and turn the heat to low for 15 minutes. Keep stirring the soup every few minutes to make sure the pasta is not sticking to each other or to the bottom of the pan.

Once the meatballs are fully cooked through, top the soup with the basil and you are ready to serve.

cheeseburger casserole

We all know what boxed food we're talking about here. It has a little hand on the front—you know the one. Well, this is a much better version of that recipe. I will say the taste brings me back to being 12 years old and sitting at school trading my food so that the other kids would give me their portion. I love the combination of beef and cheese and pasta that tastes like eating a burger in a bowl.

Makes 4–6 Servings

2 tbsp (30 ml) olive oil

1 small yellow onion, chopped

4 cloves garlic, chopped

1 lb (454 g) ground beef

1 tbsp (18 g) salt

½ tbsp (3 g) pepper

2 tsp (10 ml) Worcestershire sauce

2 tbsp (32 g) tomato paste

4 cups (940 ml) beef broth

16 oz (454 g) elbow macaroni

¾ cup (180 ml) sour cream

½ cup (120 ml) milk

3 cups (339 g) shredded cheddar cheese

In a stock pot over medium heat, add the olive oil and chopped onion and cook until translucent. Add the garlic and heat for another minute.

Add in the ground beef and season with salt and pepper. Cook the beef until no longer pink. Drain the fat and return the beef to the skillet. Add the Worcestershire sauce and tomato paste and mix.

Mix in the beef broth and add the dry macaroni. Cover the pot and bring everything to a boil over medium heat. Uncover and cook for another 5 to 7 minutes until some of the water is absorbed and the pasta is al dente. Reduce the heat to low.

Add in the sour cream and milk and stir. Once fully combined, slowly add the shredded cheddar cheese, stirring continuously. Once all the cheese is melted, cover the pot and simmer the casserole for 5 minutes before removing from the heat.

crab bake fondue

There is something fun and communal about sitting around with your family and dipping toasted bread into crab fondue while talking about your day or watching TV or discussing field trip permission slips that have not yet been signed. This recipe is one of those that you may want to double. There will be nothing left. Everyone will scoop the last little bits out of the nooks of the dish you bake it in. I'm serious; it will go fast. In fact, while writing this recipe I had to just make it real quick . . . you know, for work purposes.

Makes 4–6 Servings

8 oz (226 g) cream cheese, softened

1 cup (240 ml) mayo

2 tsp (5 g) Old Bay® seasoning

½ tsp dry mustard

½ tsp paprika

¼ cup (28 g) shredded gouda cheese

¼ cup (28 g) shredded cheddar cheese

16 oz (454 g) lump crab meat

¼ cup (12 g) chopped green onions

Preheat the oven to 350°F (176°C).

In a mixing bowl, combine the cream cheese, mayo, Old Bay seasoning, dry mustard, paprika, gouda cheese and cheddar cheese. Fold in the crab (fold it, David!) and transfer to a 3-quart (2.8-L) oven-safe baking dish.

Bake the fondue for 30 minutes, then broil it on low for 2 to 3 minutes to get a crispy brown top. Remove it from the oven and let it sit for 5 minutes before adding chopped green onions on top.

You're going to need lots of vessels to dig into this dip with. I recommend tortilla chips, but you can use crackers or even toasted bread. Thank me later.

chicken, broccoli and alfredo rice bake

When you hear chicken Alfredo, what do you think of? A pasta. Well, not here. This Chicken, Broccoli and Alfredo Rice Bake has that same delicious flavor but in a rice-based casserole. I love the broccoli in this recipe; it freshens everything up and gives a beautiful crunch in each bite. Also, peas may not be something you're used to seeing in Alfredo, but the little bits of sweetness really take this bake over the top.

Makes 4–6 Servings

1 (10-oz [283-g]) jar Alfredo sauce

½ cup (120 ml) milk

½ tsp chicken bouillon

2½ cups (500 g) uncooked white rice

2 cups (140 g) shredded rotisserie chicken

1 cup (91 g) broccoli florets, chopped

1 cup (134 g) frozen peas

½ tsp dried basil

1 cup (108 g) breadcrumbs

1 tbsp (15 ml) melted butter

Preheat the oven to 350°F (176°C).

In a bowl, mix the Alfredo sauce, milk and chicken bouillon. Add in the uncooked rice, chicken, broccoli, peas and basil. Once mixed well, transfer the mixture to a 3-quart (2.8-L) oven-safe baking dish.

Cover the baking dish with foil and bake for 30 minutes. Uncover and stir. Cover the top of the bake with the breadcrumbs and melted butter and bake uncovered for 5 more minutes to brown the breadcrumbs.

piri piri chicken with couscous

Growing up I had never heard of piri piri, ever. Then I went on my first date with my now husband to this little place called Nando's. I say this sarcastically as anyone from the U.K. knows Nando's has a cult following, and for good reason. When grilled on chicken, this spice mix gives a smoky and flavor-packed result. Pro tip: Make a lot and keep it in your spice rotation. You're going to get addicted. Your kitchen is no less than Nando's when you make this chicken. We love it over couscous but you can always pair it with rice or even mashed potatoes.

Makes 4–6 Servings

1 tsp paprika

1 tsp cumin

1 tsp oregano

¼ tsp red chili flakes

2 tbsp (28 g) butter

2 green zucchini, sliced

1 red bell pepper, chopped

2 tbsp (30 ml) olive oil

2 lb (907 g) chicken breast, cut into bite-sized pieces

1 tbsp (16 g) tomato paste

1 cup (149 g) cherry tomatoes

½ cup (120 ml) water

2 tsp (10 ml) balsamic vinegar

1 cup (173 g) couscous

Chopped basil for garnish

In a bowl, mix the paprika, cumin, oregano and chili flakes. This is your piri piri seasoning.

In a skillet over medium heat, melt the butter. Add in your zucchini and bell pepper and cook for 2 minutes until browned. Remove from the skillet and set aside.

To the same skillet, add in the olive oil and chicken and cover with the piri piri seasoning. Cook the chicken while stirring for about 7 minutes or until fully cooked through. Add in the tomato paste, cherry tomatoes and water. Bring the mixture to a boil and reduce the heat to low. After 2 to 3 minutes, or once the water has been slightly absorbed, add in the balsamic vinegar and add back in the zucchini and bell pepper.

Cook the couscous according to package directions.

Serve the chicken over the warm couscous. Top with chopped basil for garnish.

when . . .
you want
to be healthy

We have all had that moment when we walk into the house like a ravaging bear and feel like we could eat a whole bag of chips, a candy bar and a tub of ice cream and wash it down with a nice can of some sort of fizzy soda. Well, I'm here to tell you—DON'T DO IT. Not only is it going to make you feel sick, there are better and quicker options that can calm that bear down. Enter these recipes. When I used to think of healthy eating I always thought, "I'm gonna be hungry after I eat this." These recipes are not that. They will fill you up and make you feel like you are ready to start your wellness journey, right after you finish this chocolate bar. (For dessert, duh!)

skillet lasagna

This has gone viral all over the internet, and for good reason. It takes all the best parts of lasagna without the layering and baking for hours. It also holds up really well in the fridge and can be sent off the next day with whoever needs it.

Makes 4–6 Servings

2 tbsp (28 g) butter

1 yellow onion, diced

2 cloves garlic, minced

½ lb (226 g) ground beef

½ lb (226 g) ground Italian sausage

1 tbsp (18 g) salt

1 tbsp (6 g) pepper

2 tbsp (7 g) Italian seasoning

2 tbsp (32 g) tomato paste

2 cups (480 ml) marinara sauce

3 cups (720 ml) chicken broth

1 cup (240 ml) heavy cream

9 oz (255 g) broken lasagna sheets

1 cup (100 g) grated parmesan

1 cup (113 g) shredded mozzarella

¼ cup (15 g) parsley, finely chopped

¼ cup (6 g) basil, finely chopped

In a skillet over medium heat, melt the butter and add in the onions and brown till golden. Add in the garlic. Add in the beef and Italian sausage and brown for 7 to 8 minutes or until no longer pink. Season with salt, pepper and Italian seasoning and stir.

Add in the tomato paste, marinara sauce, chicken broth and heavy cream. If you are looking for a soupier consistency, you can add a little more broth at this step. Add in the pasta sheets and make sure they're covered by the broth. Cover the skillet for 5 to 7 minutes while the noodles cook.

After the noodles have cooked, remove from the heat and add in the parmesan and mozzarella. Mix until all the cheese has melted into the sauce.

Top with the parsley and basil to complete this comforting no-fuss, one-pan lasagna.

chinese chicken salad

Okay, get ready to not only make this over and over again but to make it in bulk because it can hold up in the fridge for a few days. You could also make the dressing first and put it in the bottoms of mason jars and put the dry salad on top for ready-to-shake salads in the fridge.

Makes 4–6 Servings

2 (8-oz [226-g]) bags tri-color coleslaw

2 cups (140 g) purple cabbage, chopped

2 cups (220 g) shredded carrots

1 cup (50 g) chopped green onions

1 cup (16 g) chopped cilantro

1 cup (108 g) sliced almonds

½ cup (67 g) sunflower seeds

1 pack noodles from chicken-flavored ramen

2 cups (140 g) shredded rotisserie chicken

Dressing

1 cup (240 ml) sesame oil

1-inch piece ginger, grated

2 tbsp (30 ml) garlic puree

Juice of 1 lime

¼ cup (60 ml) rice wine vinegar

¼ cup (60 ml) soy sauce

Seasoning packet from the ramen

In a bowl, combine the coleslaw, purple cabbage, carrots, green onions, cilantro, almonds and sunflower seeds.

The next step is very important. Have you had a rough day at work? Have your kids been annoying you all day? Did that driver cut you off in traffic? Take your aggression out on that packet of ramen. I use the mason jar that we're going to make the dressing in and just pound the packet of noodles. Once you're calm, open the noodle packet, set aside the seasoning packet and pour the noodles on top of the salad mix. Add the shredded chicken and set aside.

Now get your mason jar (or old pickle jar, salad shaker, or any vessel that can be shaken with a lid on top) and add in the sesame oil, ginger, garlic puree, lime juice (if you microwave the lime for 10 seconds, it will be easier to juice), rice wine vinegar, soy sauce and the ramen seasoning. Put the lid on your shaking vessel and go to town. SHAKE IT LIKE A SALTSHAKER.

Once the dressing comes together, pour it over the salad and mix well. If you want to use this salad for meal prep, pour the dressing on the bottoms of your jars and the dry salad on top and shake when ready to eat.

tortilla soup (that you'll want to make four nights a week)

Every Mexican restaurant you go to has their own version of tortilla soup. Scratch that, most *any* restaurant you go to has a version. The reason it's so popular is because it's comforting. It's a very easy and quick way to get everything you need in a bowl.

Makes 4–6 Servings

4 tbsp (60 ml) olive oil

1 yellow onion, chopped

1 red bell pepper, chopped

1 yellow bell pepper, chopped

4–5 cloves garlic, minced

1 tbsp (7 g) paprika

2 tsp (4 g) cumin

1 tbsp (8 g) chili powder

1 tsp salt

½ tsp pepper

6 cups (1440 ml) chicken broth

3 cups (210 g) shredded rotisserie chicken

1 (14.5-oz [410-g]) can diced tomatoes

1 (15-oz [425-g]) can black beans, drained and rinsed

2 cups (308 g) corn, drained

1 jalapeño, finely chopped

1 cup (16 g) chopped cilantro

8 oz (226 g) shredded Mexican cheese

Sour cream for topping

In a stock pot over medium heat, heat the olive oil and add in the chopped onion, bell peppers and garlic. Cook until everything is tender. I like to let the bell peppers sit at the bottom a little so that they get a bit of char on them; not only does it give more flavor, but it also makes the texture even better. Add in the paprika, cumin, chili powder, salt and pepper. Cook for about 1 to 2 minutes.

Add in the chicken broth, chicken, diced tomatoes, black beans, corn and jalapeño. Let this mixture simmer over low to medium heat for about 20 minutes.

I like to serve this in bowls and let everyone add the cilantro, cheese and sour cream themselves. I like a lot of cheese and a little bit of sour cream. My husband likes no cheese and lots of sour cream. The kids just want all the cheese and all the sour cream. Either way, this soup is the star of the show.

thai chicken noodle soup

There is something about noodles and soup that makes me feel like I'm being hugged. I love to sit and slurp up this noodle dish when I'm tired or it's cold outside. I don't make it spicy because I'm not a fan of spice, but you can definitely add chili oil or sriracha to the top of this soup to taste. Also, use the veggies you have in your fridge, or if you're like me, just get a bag of stir fry veggies and chop them up. You can use any rice noodles you prefer.

Makes 4–6 servings

1 (14-oz [396-g]) package thin rice noodles

Boiling water, to cover rice noodles

32 oz (960 ml) chicken stock

2 tbsp (30 g) grated ginger

1 tbsp (16 g) garlic paste

1 (13.5-oz [382-g]) can coconut milk

2 tbsp (30 ml) fish sauce

2 tbsp (30 ml) sesame oil

1 tsp turmeric

2 tbsp (30 ml) soy sauce

½ tsp sugar

1 tbsp (15 ml) lime juice

1 cup (150 g) chopped stir fry vegetables

Shredded rotisserie chicken

¼ cup (4 g) cilantro

Place the rice noodles in a bowl and cover with boiling water to cook for 10 minutes.

In a large saucepan over medium heat, combine the chicken stock, ginger and garlic and bring to a slow boil. Add in the coconut milk, fish sauce, sesame oil, turmeric, soy sauce, sugar and lime juice and stir.

Return to a boil. Add in the stir fry vegetables and let them cook for 3 to 4 minutes or until tender.

Remove from heat. Add in the shredded chicken and noodles and top with cilantro.

kani salad cucumbers

I had never heard of Kani salad until I got on TikTok and followed an amazing creator, @auntieamanda, but if you've ever had a California roll at a sushi restaurant, you're going to love this adaptation. Now, most Kani salads are a combination of these ingredients in a bowl, cut into long ribbons. This recipe really came into being because my oldest child, who could live on cucumbers, keeps a stock of English cucumbers in our fridge at all times. I use the cucumber as the edible bowl and that way there are no dishes to wash.

Makes 4–6 Servings

1 English cucumber

1 mango, diced (or 1 [12-oz (340-g)] pack of precut mangoes from the grocery store)

1 (16-oz [454-g]) package of imitation crab meat, finely chopped

For the Dressing

1 cup (240 ml) mayo

¼ cup (60 ml) sriracha

1 tsp rice wine vinegar

1 (0.35-oz [9-g]) package of seaweed sheets, optional

Okay guys, this is where your high school math classes come in handy. Peel your English cucumber and cut it into thirds. All this means is to cut it into three even pieces. Then, cut each third in half lengthwise. You should have six pieces of cucumber, seed side up. Now, take a spoon and scoop out all those seeds.

Conveniently enough, those mango slices and imitation crab sticks from the grocery store should be about the same length as your cucumber boats. Cut the mangoes and the crab into "strings" by slicing lengthwise. Top each cucumber with the sliced crab and mango.

To make the dressing, combine the mayo, sriracha and rice wine vinegar in a bowl and spoon it on top of the crab and mango mixture. Optionally, like my kids do, you can chop or rip up some seaweed sheets to top the sauce with and get that real sushi taste and texture.

broccoli salad

In all honesty, I never liked broccoli salad. I remember it was one of my mom's favorite foods. She used to get it from our local deli and just eat it all day long. I never got it. Fast-forward 20 years and not only do I snack on it all day, my kids ask me to make this all the time. There is something about the raw crunch of the broccoli and the freshness of the ingredients that makes you full, but in a healthy and satisfied way.

Makes 4–6 Servings

1 head of broccoli

1½ cups (240 g) finely chopped red onions

2 cups (226 g) shredded cheddar cheese

1 cup (112 g) chopped bacon

½ cup (26 g) chopped dill

4–5 cloves garlic, finely minced

For the Dressing

1 lime

1 cup (240 ml) mayo

½ cup (120 ml) sesame oil

2 tbsp (30 ml) Dijon mustard

1 tbsp (18 g) salt

½ tbsp (3 g) pepper

2 tbsp (13 g) celery seeds

2 tbsp (30 ml) honey

Start by removing all the florets from the head of the broccoli. I sometimes like to add a few pieces of the stalk for an extra crunch. Add the broccoli to a big bowl. Into the bowl with the broccoli, add the chopped onion, cheese, bacon, dill and garlic.

To make the dressing, microwave the lime for 10 seconds so that you can actually squeeze the juice out of it. Into a mason jar, add in all the juice from that lime with the mayo, sesame oil, Dijon mustard, salt, pepper, celery seeds and honey. Get your arm workout in and shake away to get the perfect broccoli salad dressing.

Add the dressing to the salad and it will not only be ready to eat but can also be kept in an airtight container for a week and be ready to go.

marinated avocados

I can totally see your face as you're reading the title of this recipe. Trust me when I tell you that not only is it real, but it will soon become your fave. There's something about the creaminess of the avocados over rice that is so satisfying and comforting. The crunch from the cucumber is hearty and trust me when I tell you this will knock the socks off your vegetarian friends. The key to this recipe is to start off with avocados that are not quite ready to eat.

Makes 4–6 Servings

4 firm avocados

½ English cucumber

5 cloves of garlic, minced

1–2 jalapeños, finely chopped

3 green onions, chopped

Juice from 1 lemon

For the Sauce

½ cup (120 ml) soy sauce

½ cup (120 ml) water

2 tbsp (30 ml) sesame oil

2 tbsp (30 ml) honey

1 tsp black pepper

2 tsp (8 g) black sesame seeds

First, peel, pit and cube all your avocados. Make sure to keep the chop chunky. You want good 1-inch (2.5-cm) pieces so that the sauce can really get all over the avocado. Chop the cucumber into 1-inch (2.5-cm) pieces too. Add the avocados and cucumbers into a bowl.

Add the garlic, jalapeños, green onions and lemon juice. I like to put the lemon juice on the chopped avocados and cucumbers because it keeps them from getting brown quickly.

Now, let's get ready for the magic: The sauce. To make the sauce, in a separate bowl, combine the soy sauce, water, sesame oil, honey, black pepper and sesame seeds. Mix and pour over the avocados and cucumbers. You can keep this mixture in an airtight container in the fridge for about a week.

I love to serve this over white rice and use seaweed sheets as nacho chips to scoop up the mix. Also, good luck keeping this in the fridge for a week! The longest mine has been in there before I ate it all was an hour.

refresher salad

If you ever needed a reason to just sit on the couch and chomp on crunchy greens, this is it. My kids love this salad to the point where they will ask for it for movie nights because the crunchy vibes are so satisfying. If you went to a healthy grocery store and bought a little bowl of this salad, it would easily cost you $12–15. Make it at home, and you can not only get a vat full for around $7–10, but you can also feed the whole family (and your neighbors).

Makes 6–8 Servings

1 head of purple cabbage

1 cup (48 g) chopped green onions

1 cup (60 g) chopped parsley

1 cup (16 g) chopped cilantro

2 cups (260 g) shaved Brussels sprouts (or finely chopped Brussels sprouts)

2 cups (340 g) cooked shrimp or shredded chicken

For the Dressing

½ cup (120 ml) olive oil

¼ cup (60 ml) apple cider vinegar

⅓ cup (80 ml) soy sauce

1 tbsp (16 g) peanut butter

2 tbsp (30 ml) honey

¼ tbsp black pepper

1 tbsp (7 g) paprika

Start by chopping the cabbage. I like to make it into strands; that way it feels like eating noodles. But I also like to do a chop and eat the end result with a spoon. Put the cabbage into a bowl. Add in green onions, parsley, cilantro, shaved Brussels sprouts and shrimp or chicken.

To make the dressing, use an extra large mason jar. I use this because if it's just me eating, I pour the dressing only on my bowl and then save the rest for when I'm going to eat later. Add the olive oil, apple cider vinegar, soy sauce, peanut butter, honey, black pepper and paprika. Shake vigorously until the peanut butter is fully combined.

strawberry cucumber salad

Okay, before you put this down, I know how it sounds. I was never really a fruit-in-my-salad person, but for some reason this doesn't seem like fruit in salad but more like a salad of fruit. The savory, sweet and spicy flavors make one of the most satisfying combinations, especially in summer when Florida can get up to a hundred degrees in the shade. This is one of those salads you're going to want to eat with a spoon because a fork just doesn't shovel enough in your mouth. I also love to grab a bag of tortilla chips and put this salad on the counter, because magically the kids will scoop this all day long.

Makes 4–6 Servings

3 cups (432 g) strawberries

1 English cucumber

8–10 radishes

1–3 jalapeños, finely chopped

1 cup (16 g) chopped cilantro

2 green onions, chopped

1 lemon

1 lime

½ tsp salt

¼ tsp celery seeds

The key to this recipe is to get ready to finely chop everything. I use a straw to poke through the bottom of the strawberry and remove the leaves all the way without losing half of the strawberry by cutting the tops off. This is also a really good and knife-free way for the kids to help in the kitchen. After you remove all the leaves, cut about four slices horizontally and four slices vertically—that's about how small you want your chop.

Next, chop the cucumber and radishes to about the same size. I like to slice the jalapeño vertically and remove the seeds and the ribs before chopping finely, just because I don't like mine too spicy. If your spice tolerance is higher than mine (when I tell you everyone in the world's is), you can skip the removal of the guts.

Add the strawberries, cucumbers and radishes to a bowl. Add in the cilantro and green onions. I like to add in both the green and white parts of the onions because I think they round out the flavors better.

Finally, you're going to stick the lemon and lime in the microwave for about 10 seconds so you can actually get all the juice out of them because you're going to need every drop. Add in all the juice to the bowl, top with salt and celery seeds and mix.

shrimp and corn salad

This is the easiest and freshest shrimp salad to exist. I use Bibb or butter lettuce as taco cups and eat so many before actually getting everything to the table for the family. Shh, don't tell anyone. You can make this in the summer with fresh corn on the cob, but I crave this year-round and use organic sweet kernel corn in a can and I swear it tastes the same, if not better. Also, get the already cooked shrimp from the seafood department in the grocery store to save time.

Makes 4–6 Servings

2 cups (202 g) roughly chopped celery

2 cups (266 g) roughly chopped cucumbers

2 avocados, roughly chopped

1 jalapeño, finely chopped

1 cup (50 g) chopped green onions

1 cup (16 g) chopped cilantro

¼ cup (48 g) capers

2 cups (308 g) canned corn, drained

3 cups (510 g) cooked shrimp

1 cup (240 ml) olive oil

1 lemon

2 tbsp (32 g) garlic paste

1 tbsp (14 g) anchovy paste

1 tbsp (18 g) salt

½ tbsp (3 g) pepper

1 tbsp (7 g) celery seeds

Bibb lettuce

Add the celery, cucumbers and avocados to a bowl. You can remove the seeds and ribs from the jalapeño or leave them if you like it spicy. Add in the green onions (both green and white parts), cilantro and capers.

Next, open and drain your cans of corn. I like to run them under cold water just to get that "canned" taste off and make them taste a little cleaner. If you're using fresh corn, take it off the cob and boil it in water to cook the kernels. Add the corn to the bowl.

Rinse the shrimp to take off that seafood-counter smell. Chop each shrimp into four to five little pieces, and add to the bowl of greens and corn.

To make the dressing, to any vessel that you can cover and shake, add in the olive oil, lemon, garlic paste, anchovy paste, salt, pepper and celery seeds. Shake together for your perfect fresh dressing. Add the dressing to the salad and scoop into Bibb lettuce leaves.

mexican street corn salad

Though this recipe isn't authentic, it is a true bowl of warm and satisfying freshness. If you're making this in summer, try to find and use some real good fresh ears of corn. However, I actually do use the organic canned corn all year round so either way, you're in good hands.

Makes 4–6 Servings

½ cup (120 ml) olive oil

2 tbsp (28 g) butter

2 tbsp (17 g) garlic, chopped

12 oz (340 g) fresh or frozen corn

½ tbsp (9 g) salt

½ tbsp (3 g) pepper

½ tbsp (3 g) paprika

¼ cup (60 ml) mayo

¼ cup (60 ml) sour cream

2 tbsp (30 ml) lime juice

½ cup (50 g) freshly grated parmesan cheese

1 cup (16 g) chopped cilantro

1 cup (50 g) chopped green onions

1½ cups (240 g) finely chopped red onions

1 jalapeño, finely chopped

½ cup (60 g) cotija cheese

Into a skillet over medium heat, add the olive oil and butter. People always ask why I do both. The butter is for the taste and the oil is for the temperature. Add the garlic and get it nice and warmed up until it's golden but not too brown.

Add in the corn and mix for about 5 to 6 minutes or until it's tender and golden. Season the cooked corn with the salt, pepper and paprika. Cook for another minute to get all the seasoning incorporated.

Transfer the warm corn to a heat-safe bowl and add the mayo, sour cream, lime juice, parmesan cheese, cilantro, green onions, red onions and jalapeño. Mix. Once everything is incorporated, top with the cotija cheese.

I love to toast some bread and top it with this mix, or eat it with just a massive bag of tortilla chips. Your heart will show you the way forward.

tomato fish soup

This recipe comes from as close to my heart as possible. My Nani (grandmother) makes this and it is an all-time favorite for everyone we know. Not only is it our family fave, but when I got married and made it for my husband, it instantly became his favorite too. The best part of this recipe is that it is so super easy and comes together in less than 15 minutes on the stove. There is a catch: if you don't like cilantro and have the soap genotype, this is not the recipe for you. Cilantro is the key to this fish. On the other hand, if you are a cilantro lover, make this ASAP!

Makes 4–6 Servings

6 plum tomatoes

1 lb (454 g) cod filets (or any white fish you like)

¼ cup (60 ml) olive oil

¼ cup (34 g) finely chopped garlic

½ cup (132 g) tomato paste

32 oz (960 ml) vegetable broth

2 cups (32 g) chopped cilantro

Before you start cooking, chop up your tomatoes into ½-inch (1-cm) pieces and your fish into about 2-inch (5-cm) pieces.

Into a stock pot over medium heat, add the olive oil. As the oil is warming, add the garlic just for about 10 to 15 seconds; you're not trying to get color on it—you just want it to infuse into the olive oil.

Add the chopped tomatoes and cook for 5 to 7 minutes or until the tomatoes fall apart. Add in your tomato paste and mix. Once you have a thick base, add in your vegetable broth. Once the broth comes to a boil, turn the heat to low and add in your fish pieces. Make sure all the fish is submerged in the broth. Once you place the fish in the broth, don't mix it or move the pieces around. If you don't let them cook in the broth first, the fish will fall apart.

Cover your stock pot and cook the fish for 15 minutes over low heat. Once the fish is cooked through, uncover and add in your cilantro. Carefully fold it in and mix everything together.

I love this fish over rice, but trust me when I tell you that when I'm hungry I can eat it straight up out of a bowl.

cabbage corn salad

I don't really like to call this a salad. This meal is hearty, filling and super delicious. Because it uses cabbage instead of any type of lettuce, it can hold up in lunch boxes all day and in the fridge for days without getting soggy or watery. I find it funny that this "salad" has shown up in so many of my other meals. I have topped fish tacos with it, I have added it to taco bowls and I have eaten it out of Tupperware® while standing in front of my fridge after the kids have gone to sleep and I needed a snack. Get ready to make this a lot; it'll become a fan favorite before you know it.

Makes 6–8 Servings

1 head of cabbage, finely chopped

1–2 jalapeños

2 (15.25-oz [432-g]) cans sweet corn

2 green onions

1 cup (16 g) cilantro

For the Dressing

Juice of 1 lime

2 tbsp (30 ml) sesame oil

1 cup (240 ml) mayo

2 tbsp (30 ml) grainy mustard

2 tbsp (13 g) celery seeds

1 tbsp (18 g) salt

½ tbsp (3 g) pepper

¼ tsp sugar

Place the chopped cabbage into a bowl. Next, you're going to chop the jalapeños, finely, like as fine as you can go. If you need to make it less spicy, make sure to cut down the middle and take out the seeds before you chop. The hard part about chopping a jalapeño is making sure you don't touch your eyes after.

Next, drain your two cans of corn and add to the bowl. Finally, chop your green onions and cilantro and mix them right in. If you are one of those people who thinks that cilantro tastes like soap, please omit this ingredient.

To make the dressing, add the juice of 1 lime, sesame oil, mayo, grainy mustard, celery seeds, salt, pepper and sugar to any jar (nothing fancy; I use a mason jar) and shake that sucker for about 30 seconds. Voilà! Just like that you have a delicious homemade dressing.

Top the salad with the dressing and get ready to taste summer and happiness in one bite.

chicken and sweet corn soup

This recipe is super near and dear to my heart. This is actually the first recipe my mom taught me how to make. If you've ever heard of Indo-Chinese food, this is the staple recipe: the best of both Indian and Chinese food. This soup is thick and creamy without cream and so satisfying to have after a long week. When I was a kid, this was a Sunday night staple. The funny part is, once she taught me how to make it, it became my job every Sunday to feed the family. Recently, she made it for my kids when they were spending the weekend with her and called me to make sure the recipe was correct because she hadn't made it in so many years. This is a full-circle-to-my-heart recipe. I add chicken to it; you can very easily leave it out and make it vegetarian, or take it a step further and either add shrimp or pork, depending on your preference.

Makes 4–6 Servings

2 (14.75-oz [396-g]) cans creamed corn

30 oz (900 ml) vegetable broth

1 tsp salt

1 tsp sugar

3 tbsp (24 g) cornstarch

5 tbsp (75 ml) water

1 beaten egg

2 tsp (10 ml) soy sauce

1 rotisserie chicken, shredded

3–4 green onions to garnish

To a stock pot, add the two cans of creamed corn and equal parts vegetable stock before you turn the heat on the stove. Combine, then add in the salt and the sugar. Bring to a slow boil over medium heat.

While you're waiting for the pot to boil, mix together the cornstarch and water to make a slurry. I keep the slurry and the beaten egg right next to the pot because once it boils, everything goes really quickly. As soon as you see a boil happening, add the slurry and mix it through the soup. Instantly you will see the soup thicken. Next is the most fun part. Hold the bowl with the beaten egg about 1 foot (30 cm) above the soup pot and slowly stream the egg into the soup while at the same time mixing the soup with a wood spoon/spatula. Once finished, you will see gorgeous ribbons of egg floating in the soup. Add in the soy sauce and shredded rotisserie chicken and mix through.

Slice your green onions at an angle and use for garnish when you put the soup in bowls. Tell me you don't feel like you're sitting in a fancy Chinese or Indian restaurant after you taste this.

when . . .
you haven't gone
grocery shopping

There are so many times when the last grocery haul runs out at our house. We try to put random things that are left in the fridge together to make something that we want to eat. You know what they say—necessity is the mother of invention. It is a necessity to feed the people that live in your house, but sometimes there's no time to stop at the grocery store. So, let's get started making full meals with those little bits left around the kitchen.

baked chicken, broccoli and corn casserole

This is one of the easiest dump, mix and bake recipes around. You can actually even prep all this in the morning and leave it in the fridge and tell your kids or partner to stick it in the oven whenever they get home. I'm not promising that they will do it or that you will actually prep it in the morning before leaving the house, but we can all wish and pretend we have it all together like that. I don't have it all together, ever. That's why when I actually do get home and can't stand to do anything else for the day and have to feed four other mouths besides my own, this is usually my go-to.

Makes 4–6 Servings

2 tbsp (28 g) butter

I rotisserie chicken, shredded

12 oz (340 g) broccoli florets

8 oz (226 g) cream cheese

I oz (28 g) ranch seasoning mix

I cup (112 g) chopped bacon

8 oz (226 g) shredded cheddar cheese

16 oz (480 ml) sour cream

12 oz (340 g) frozen corn

2 tbsp (17 g) garlic powder

2 tbsp (14 g) paprika

I tbsp (12 g) Cajun seasoning

I jalapeño, chopped

3 green onions, sliced

Preheat your oven to 400°F (205°C). Spread the butter all over a 3-quart (2.8-L) oven-safe baking dish.

In a mixing bowl, combine the rotisserie chicken, broccoli florets, cream cheese, ranch seasoning, bacon, cheddar cheese, sour cream, frozen corn, garlic powder, paprika, Cajun seasoning and jalapeño. Mix and spread evenly into the baking dish.

Cover the dish with foil. At this point you can either stick it in the fridge (if you are one of those above-mentioned people who have their life together early in the morning or days in advance) and keep it safe until you're ready to bake it, or if you're like me and you're reading and doing this about half an hour before everyone has to eat, you can stick it in the oven for 30 minutes and get ready to eat.

Remove the foil and top with the sliced green onions before serving.

pizza biscuit puffs

When I was a kid and I got home from school, my go-to snack was Hot Pockets®. I loved them. Like truly loved them. Once I had my own kids, I started making them at home. I will toot my own horn here and say that these are so much better than what I ate as a kid. The fun part is that you can let each kid add in what they like and it gets them in the kitchen and more aware of flavors that they like. If you have a kid who's like one of mine, it will still always just be cheese and sauce. There's no problem with that. It's the retro classic love for me. Also, just as Hot Pockets were always convenient and in the freezer ready to go, this recipe can be as well. Make a whole bunch on a weekend and put the flavors per kid in a freezer storage bag with their name on it. That way each kid knows which ones are theirs.

Makes 4–6 Servings

1 (16-oz [454-g]) tube Grands!™ Flaky Layers Original Biscuits

14 oz (420 ml) pizza sauce

16 oz (454 g) sliced mozzarella cheese

2 tbsp (6 g) oregano

Optional Toppings

Mushrooms

Olives

Pepperoni

Pineapple

Green peppers

Onions

Ham

Preheat an air fryer to 320°F (160°C) or an oven to 350°F (176°C).

The first and hardest step of this process is to pop that biscuit package and take years off your life by scaring yourself. Once you get past this, take each biscuit and split it in half horizontally. Next you can either take a rolling pin and spread them out a bit, or use your fingers and spread the biscuits flat.

You're going to top one side of the biscuit with pizza sauce, cheese and oregano, and any other toppings you want. Once you are satisfied with everything in your personal pocket, cover with the other half of the biscuit and crimp the edges with a fork, making sure you have sealed the pocket all the way around.

Now if you live off an air fryer like I do, stick it in that bad boy for 8 minutes. If you haven't crossed over to the air frying cult as of yet, you can just put them in the oven for 8 to 10 minutes until golden brown.

boursin veggie pasta

If you were on TikTok during the pandemic, you saw the viral pastas that were taking over our world. This is a version of those recipes but the amount of flavor packed into this pasta is insane. The best part is that you can adjust this recipe to whatever is left in your fridge. We have put asparagus into this, my husband likes to add celery . . . honestly the possibilities are endless. The most important part is the cheese. That pat of cheese really makes this pasta.

Makes 4–6 Servings

8 oz (226 g) rotini pasta

5.2 oz (147 g) shallot and chive Boursin cheese

12 oz (340 g) steamed broccoli florets

1½ cups (165 g) shredded carrots

2 cups (308 g) canned corn, drained

1 cup (30 g) baby spinach

½ cup (27 g) sun-dried tomatoes

4–5 cloves garlic, minced

¼ cup (60 ml) olive oil

1 tsp salt

½ tsp pepper

1 tsp paprika

¼ cup (60 ml) pasta water

Parmesan cheese, grated (for topping)

Cook your pasta according to package instructions. Make sure to add salt to the water when you make your pasta. Drain pasta, reserving ¼ cup (60 ml) of the pasta water.

Preheat your oven to 400°F (205°C).

Into the middle of a 3-quart (2.8-L) oven-safe dish, add the Boursin cheese. You don't need to spread it or move it. Leave it whole and add the broccoli, carrots, corn, spinach, sun-dried tomatoes and garlic all around the cheese.

Top everything with the olive oil and season with the salt, pepper and paprika. Bake for 25 minutes.

Add the cooked pasta directly to the dish as soon as it comes out of the oven. Mix and add in the pasta water as needed to help the dish come together. Top the pasta with parmesan cheese as you plate per person.

mushroom hash brown bake

There is something to be said for switching up meal times. This sounds like it would be a great breakfast or brunch meal (which it can be and I'm sure has been), but making this for dinner keeps everyone on their toes. If you really want to get fancy and show off your skills, you can always do sunny-side-up eggs on top of each person's plate or even just make a few and put them on top of the casserole. Also, try to think of this bake as a massive pie with a hash brown crust. That's right, I said it—a hash brown crust of goodness.

Makes 4–6 Servings

12 frozen hash browns

2 tbsp (28 g) butter

4–5 cloves garlic, minced

1 lb (454 g) ground Italian sausage

16 oz (454 g) sliced mushrooms

1 tsp salt

½ tsp black pepper

16 oz (454 g) baby spinach

8 oz (226 g) shredded cheddar cheese

3 tbsp (9 g) finely chopped chives

Preheat your oven to 375°F (190°C).

Line the bottom of a 3-quart (2.8-L) oven-safe dish with your frozen hash browns. Bake for 20 minutes, flipping the hash browns halfway through. Take the hash browns out and set aside.

While your hash browns are in the oven, heat a skillet over medium heat. Add in the butter and garlic, and brown. Add in the ground Italian sausage and cook until there is no pink left. Add in mushrooms and sauté until they get some color on them. Season with the salt and pepper and add in the spinach. It will only take about 1 to 2 minutes for the spinach to wilt into the meat.

Return the hash browns to the bottom of the baking dish. Add the sausage mixture on top of your hash browns and top with the shredded cheddar cheese. Stick back in the oven for 4 to 5 minutes just so the cheese melts all over the meat. Remove from the oven, top with chopped chives and serve right away.

one pot broccoli pasta

When I originally made it kind of big on social media, I was known for my dump cake desserts. If there is an equivalent savory dish, this is the one. You won't believe that this is a thing, but you can truly boil everything in one pot, like you usually would do to cook just pasta, and have a hearty meal ready. I used to just add the onions directly to the broth to cook, but I realized I liked it better when I cooked the onions first, so this is the final version and it does not disappoint. I like broccoli because it gets nice and soft and because my kids could live on it, but I have done this with asparagus and even green beans when I didn't feel like going to the grocery store.

Makes 4–6 Servings

2 tbsp (30 ml) olive oil

1 yellow onion, chopped

4–5 cloves garlic, minced

32 oz (960 ml) chicken broth

2 cups (480 ml) heavy cream

16 oz (454 g) rotini pasta

1½ cups (137 g) broccoli florets

1 tbsp (7 g) red pepper flakes

1 tsp salt

½ tsp pepper

½ cup (50 g) freshly grated parmesan cheese

Into a stock pot over medium heat, add the olive oil and sauté the onion until translucent. Add the garlic and cook for just about 1 minute; you don't want to get too much color on the garlic.

Add in the chicken broth, heavy cream, pasta, broccoli, red pepper flakes, salt and pepper. Bring to a boil, then reduce to low/medium and cover the pot with a lid. Keep on the heat for 12 to 15 minutes until all the liquid is absorbed.

Remove from the heat and mix in the parmesan cheese.

southwest chicken

This recipe—please don't judge me—was made by accident. I was actually going to make a veggie pasta and between answering my kids' math homework questions, answering the phone that had been ringing for a while and my husband breaking the towel rack in our bathroom upstairs (I heard a crash), I messed up and put in the chicken that was supposed to be for lunch boxes the next day. So, here we are. This meal is so hearty and asked for on repeat. Like most things in our life, it was just meant to be.

Makes 4–6 Servings

2 tbsp (30 ml) olive oil

1 shallot or small yellow onion, chopped

4–5 cloves garlic, finely minced

2 yellow squashes

1 red bell pepper, chopped

1 cup (154 g) sweet corn kernels, drained

1 tsp salt

1 tsp pepper

2 tbsp (32 g) tomato paste

¼ cup (60 ml) hot water

2 tbsp (24 g) Cajun seasoning

1 rotisserie chicken, shredded

1 cup (16 g) chopped cilantro

1 lime, optional

Shredded cheese, optional

Into a skillet over medium heat, add the olive oil, shallots and garlic. Cook for 3 to 4 minutes. Add in the yellow squash, red bell pepper and corn and season with the salt and pepper. Cook for only another minute or 2 until the veggies are tender.

Add in the tomato paste and hot water and combine. Season with the Cajun seasoning and stir to combine.

Fold in the rotisserie chicken and top with the cilantro. My husband likes to add a squeeze of fresh lime; I on the other hand add a handful of cheese. Either option will make you close your eyes and savor the party in your mouth at first bite.

mushroom pappardelle pasta

The key to this recipe is to use really good ingredients for the sauce. I get organic heavy cream, the best mushrooms and fresh parmesan cheese. To get your dish to look and taste restaurant-quality, finish the sauce with the water from cooking the pasta. This gives it the creaminess and the finished "something" you're missing at home. You can also always add any protein to this meal, but I like just the mushroom taste. I also sometimes add extra mushrooms, like a lot. What can I say, I'm a mushroom kind of girl.

Makes 4–6 Servings

16 oz (454 g) pappardelle noodles

2 tbsp (30 ml) olive oil

1 tbsp (14 g) butter

1 yellow onion, chopped

4–5 cloves garlic, finely minced

16 oz (454 g) sliced baby bella mushrooms

1 tbsp (18 g) salt

½ tbsp (3 g) pepper

1 tbsp (7 g) paprika

1½ cups (360 ml) heavy cream

1½ tbsp (18 g) Cajun seasoning

¼ cup (60 ml) pasta water

½ cup (50 g) grated parmesan cheese

Fill a pot with water and salt it like ocean water. Bring to a boil. Place your noodles in the water and cook al dente (according to package directions).

Into a skillet over medium heat, add the olive oil and butter, making sure to melt and not burn the butter. Add in the chopped onions and cook till translucent. Add the garlic and heat for about a minute, not getting too much color on the garlic.

Wipe down your mushrooms with a damp cloth to remove any dirt, but make sure you are not submerging them in water to wash them, as they will absorb the water and not cook well. Add the mushrooms to the skillet with the onions, and sauté till they are cooked down and browned. Season with the salt, pepper and paprika. Cook for 1 to 2 minutes.

Add in the heavy cream and season with the Cajun seasoning. Mix and bring to a boil. Once everything is incorporated and boiling, reduce to medium heat, add in the cooked noodles and toss. Add the pasta water as needed to make the sauce creamy and restaurant-like. Top with the parmesan cheese and you are ready to eat!

no-fry sweet and sour chicken

For most sweet and sour chicken recipes, you have to coat and fry the chicken first to give it that crunch and candied taste. I am not a fan. When I was a kid, we used to have sweet and sour chicken at our favorite Chinese restaurant (August Moon, which sadly no longer exists) and they made it without the fry. So, when I got older and ate this meal at other restaurants, I never understood the thick coating. This is my take on it without the fry. If you are not a fan, you are more than welcome to fry up some chicken and then continue on with the rest of the recipe.

Makes 4–6 Servings

2 lb (907 g) chicken breast

1 tsp salt

½ tsp pepper

¾ cup (150 g) granulated sugar

½ cup (120 ml) apple cider vinegar

¼ cup (60 ml) ketchup

2 tbsp (30 ml) soy sauce

1 tbsp (15 ml) sesame oil

Cut the chicken into 1-inch (2.5-cm) pieces and season with the salt and pepper. Set aside in a bowl. In a measuring cup or separate bowl, whisk together the sugar, apple cider vinegar, ketchup, soy sauce and sesame oil until the sugar is fully dissolved. Set aside.

In a skillet over medium heat, melt 2 tablespoons (28 g) of the butter. Add in the chicken pieces and cook for 8 to 10 minutes until all the chicken is browned and cooked through. Remove the chicken from the pan and put into a new clean bowl. Set aside.

4 tbsp (57 g) butter, divided

3–4 cloves garlic, finely chopped

1 small yellow onion, chopped

1 red bell pepper, chopped

1 green bell pepper, chopped

1 cup (165 g) pineapple chunks

1 tbsp (8 g) cornstarch, mixed with 2 tbsp (30 ml) water to make a slurry

Into the same pan, add 2 tablespoons (28 g) of the butter, garlic, onions, red bell pepper and green bell pepper. Sauté for 5 to 7 minutes or until the peppers are tender. Add in the pineapple and cook for 1 more minute just to warm up the pineapple.

Add in the prepared mix of sugar, apple cider vinegar, ketchup, soy sauce and sesame oil and lower the heat to a simmer. Once simmering, add in the cornstarch slurry to thicken your sauce. Add back in your chicken and mix everything well.

I love this over white rice, but my husband prefers it over quinoa. Either way, I think it's better than the fried version and hope you love it as much as I do.

deviled egg pasta

I am going to be super honest and transparent with you guys. I hate eggs. This recipe is featured in this book because everyone in my life and in my house is obsessed with eggs and I've been told this is their favorite egg meal. I actually learned this recipe from a chef who used to make brown bag lunches for grown-ups who worked around the building where he lived.

Makes 6–8 Servings

6 eggs

8 oz (226 g) small pasta (I use ditalini)

¾ cup (180 ml) mayo

1½ tbsp (22 ml) Dijon mustard

2 cloves garlic, finely minced

1 cup (160 g) chopped red onions

1 tbsp (18 g) salt

½ tbsp (3 g) paprika

¼ tsp chili powder

1 tbsp (7 g) celery seeds

¼ cup (13 g) chopped dill

3 green onions, chopped

Into a medium pot, add the eggs and enough water to cover the eggs by at least 1 inch (2.5 cm). Place the pot over high heat and set a timer for 11 minutes. Once the timer rings, drain the water and pour cold tap water over the eggs in the pot to stop them cooking. Peel the eggs and let them cool.

As your eggs are cooling, cook the pasta in salted water according to package directions. You can use bigger pasta if you like, but there's just something about the little pasta that I feel makes it more fun and easier to eat.

Once you can handle them, chop the eggs between a fine and medium chop. Add the chopped eggs into a bowl. To the bowl, add the mayo, mustard, garlic, red onion, salt, paprika, chili powder, celery seeds, cooked pasta and dill. Fold everything together, keeping the eggs as intact as possible. Garnish with the green onions and a little sprinkle of paprika on top.

seven-layer mediterranean chicken dip

This recipe went super viral on my TikTok early on. The funny part is that it was originally intended to be a Super Bowl party recipe. You must be thinking: How can this "dip" be included in a recipe book for dinner? Well, my family started obsessing over it and wanted it all the time. So, it eventually evolved into somewhat of a gyro chicken sandwich. Let me tell you, I've sent it in my kids' lunch boxes and it is the one sandwich that has never come back home. The pita pockets are so easy to fill and not messy to eat, as nothing falls out of the bottom.

Makes 4–6 Servings

10 oz (283 g) roasted garlic hummus

10 oz (283 g) spinach artichoke dip

1 English cucumber

2 cups (360 g) sliced Kalamata olives

2 cups (480 g) roasted red peppers, chopped

1 cup (160 g) chopped red onions

8 oz (226 g) crumbled feta cheese

¼ cup (13 g) fresh dill, chopped

In a 9 x 13–inch (23 x 33–cm) dish, lay down an even layer of the hummus. I buy mine, but if you want to make your own, more power to ya. I just feel like my local grocer has some really good hummus and it saves me time, money and effort.

Then, layer the spinach artichoke dip on top of the hummus. (I also buy this at the deli.)

Finely chop the English cucumber and spread evenly over the spinach and artichoke dip. Next, add the Kalamata olives. I buy them already sliced. Make sure to get the Kalamata olives—for some reason black olives don't hit the same and take away from the flavor of the overall meal. Next, layer on the chopped roasted red peppers, red onions and crumbled feta cheese. Top with fresh chopped dill and voilà! The hard part is all done.

4–6 pieces pita bread

I rotisserie chicken, shredded and warmed

Pepperoncinis, optional

Now for the fun part: Cut a pita in half and split open the middle. Take a healthy scoop or two of the layered dip and spread it into the pita. Add the rotisserie chicken. I like to take a bite of the sandwich and then take a bite of a pepperoncini to have a Greek party in my mouth.

baked spinach and ricotta shells

My Italian friend taught me something amazing. You know when you buy those lasagna noodle boxes that say you don't need to cook them first? That's just a marketing tactic. You actually don't have to cook any dry pasta before baking it, as long as you're putting it into a liquid, or in this case, lots and lots of sauce. Have you ever tried to stuff a giant shell noodle once it's cooked? It is not fun. At all. This technique makes it so easy to stuff shells that you can make this once super-complicated meal during the week. Also, get those kids to stuff the shells. They love it, and it's less work for you.

Makes 4–6 Servings

15 oz (425 g) ricotta cheese

10 oz (283 g) chopped frozen spinach, thawed

1 egg

2 tbsp (36 g) salt

2 tbsp (13 g) pepper

¼ tsp nutmeg

12 oz (340 g) large shell pasta

2 (24–oz [680–ml]) jars marinara sauce

2 cups (226 g) shredded mozzarella cheese

2 tbsp (7 g) Italian seasoning

1 cup (24 g) fresh basil

Preheat the oven to 350°F (176°C). Make sure you do this first. I always forget. This is me telling you: Don't forget.

In a mixing bowl, combine the ricotta, spinach, egg, salt, pepper and nutmeg. Mix everything well. This will be the filling for our shells. Add the mixture to each dry pasta shell, making sure each shell is totally full of the mixture. Scrape the top of each shell so the filling is flat and not coming out of the shell.

Lay the shells in a single layer in a 3-quart (2.8-L) oven-safe baking dish. You do not need to grease the pan as the sauce will provide enough moisture for nothing to stick. Speaking of sauce, add the marinara sauce to make sure all the shells are submerged and there is enough sauce to cover the top. I know it looks like a lot, but remember our shells are not cooked, and this sauce is going to cook them.

Cover the baking dish (I just use foil) and bake for 1 hour. Remove from the oven and add shredded mozzarella cheese. Sprinkle the Italian seasoning on top of the cheese. Put the dish back into the oven for 15 minutes or until the cheese is golden and bubbling. Remove and top with basil. Pro tip—have garlic bread ready on the side. You will need it to sop up the sauce.

salmon in garlic cream sauce

I had a dish like this in West Palm Beach, Florida, and ever since have been obsessed with re-creating it. I like to buy a big slab of salmon from Costco and then cut it into filets the size I like. Everything comes together in one pan and the hardest part of this dish is not eating the whole salmon before you feed your family.

Makes 4–6 Servings

4–6 salmon filets

4–6 tbsp (60–90 ml) olive oil

4 tsp (24 g) salt, divided

4 tsp (8 g) pepper, divided

1½ tsp (4 g) crushed red pepper

1 tsp paprika

4 tbsp (56 g) butter

6–8 cloves garlic

2 cups (480 ml) chicken broth

1 cup (240 ml) heavy cream

4 tbsp (58 g) cream cheese

3 tbsp (11 g) Italian seasoning

2 cups (60 g) baby spinach

2 tbsp (6 g) chives

Parmesan cheese for topping

2 tbsp (3 g) fresh basil, torn

On a cutting board, rub the salmon filets with olive oil and season with 2 teaspoons (12 g) salt, 2 teaspoons (4 g) pepper, crushed red pepper and paprika. Rub the spices onto the salmon and set aside.

In a pan over medium heat, melt the butter. Place the salmon in the pan and cook for about 5 minutes on each side until cooked through. Take the salmon out of the pan and set aside on a plate.

Add the garlic to the same pan and warm it up without getting too much color on it. Once your garlic is golden, add in the chicken broth, heavy cream and cream cheese and mix well until there are no lumps. Season your cream sauce with 2 teaspoons (12 g) salt, 2 teaspoons (4 g) pepper and Italian seasoning and mix. Add spinach and chives and mix till the spinach is wilted.

Place the salmon back in the pan with the sauce and let it simmer for about 5 minutes. Top with freshly grated parmesan cheese and torn basil and get ready for people to ask you, "You made this?!"

when . . .
you haven't done the dishes

In our house, we have come to a very comfortable arrangement. I cook. He cleans. I hate doing the dishes and it's only fair that if I'm making all the food, everyone else needs to clean up the kitchen. Well, sometimes when everyone is exhausted and things are in the dishwasher and the dishwasher hasn't been run yet, there's a backlog. In those times, I *could* be the helper and do all the dishes before I start making dinner. But who are we kidding? I am going to find the one clean pot or pan and make dinner in that. Not only will these recipes be delicious, but they will also make everyone want to finish all the dishes tonight or else tomorrow we're getting takeout.

spinach artichoke dip chicken bake

The one thing I will forever order as an appetizer when I go out to eat is a hot spinach and artichoke dip. Now imagine that amazing creamy flavor over a baked chicken. This recipe is so simple that you don't even have to cook the chicken first. The spinach dip makes the chicken super soft and moist and adds so much flavor.

Makes 4–6 Servings

4 boneless chicken breasts

8 oz (226 g) cream cheese, room temperature

½ cup (120 ml) sour cream

¼ cup (60 ml) heavy cream

6 oz (170 g) frozen spinach, thawed

1 (14-oz [396-g]) can artichoke hearts, chopped

5 oz (142 g) crumbled feta cheese

1 cup (160 g) chopped yellow onions

4–5 cloves garlic, chopped

½ tsp salt

½ tsp pepper

1 tbsp (7 g) paprika

1 tsp red pepper flakes

1 tbsp (4 g) Italian seasoning

1 cup (100 g) grated parmesan cheese

Preheat the oven to 375°F (190°C).

Spray a 3-quart (2.8-L) oven-safe baking dish with nonstick cooking spray. Add the raw chicken to the pan and set aside.

In a mixing bowl, combine the cream cheese, sour cream, heavy cream, defrosted frozen spinach, chopped artichokes, feta cheese, yellow onion, chopped garlic, salt, pepper, paprika, red pepper flakes and Italian seasoning.

Spread the mix over the raw chicken in an even layer and bake for 50 minutes. Remove and spread the cream cheese mixture around. Top with parmesan cheese and bake for another 5 to 10 minutes until the top is browned.

Serve with crusty toasted French bread; you're going to need it.

chicken chili

This recipe is so versatile. I keep it in my back pocket as a base for so many quick meals during the week. All you need is a spoon to dig into this meal that tastes like it's been on the stove all day. If you have tortillas, you've got yourself a taco night. Add some pasta and you've got an Italian feast ready for the whole family. How do I know all this? I've made both of these with the leftovers of this one pot chicken chili.

Makes 4–6 Servings

2 tbsp (30 ml) olive oil

1 medium yellow onion, chopped

3 cloves garlic, chopped

1 (15-oz [425-g]) can black beans

¼ tsp salt

1 lb (454 g) ground chicken

1 oz (28 g) taco seasoning

⅔ cup (160 ml) water

16 oz (454 g) restaurant-style salsa

1 cup (136 g) frozen corn

For the Toppings

Sour cream

Avocado

Cheese

Green onions

Jalapeños

Cilantro

Into a medium saucepan over medium heat, add the olive oil and sauté the onions and garlic until the onions are translucent. While you're waiting for the onions to cook, open your black beans, drain them and rinse them with water. Set them aside until ready to use.

Once the onions are cooked through, add the salt and get ready for the action. To your onions, add the ground chicken, and brown through. There should be no pink left on the chicken. Now, here is the kicker: Do not drain the fat. Trust me when I tell you this—don't do it. Once the chicken is browned, add the taco seasoning and ⅔ cup (160 ml) water, and cook over medium for about 5 minutes or until the seasoning and water are absorbed into the chicken.

From here, you're almost ready to eat. Get ready because it's going to go fast. Add the salsa, the drained and rinsed black beans and corn to the chicken mixture. Mix thoroughly and cook over medium heat for 5 to 7 minutes.

Enjoy your chili with any of your favorite toppings! (I like sour cream, cilantro, cheese and green onions.) Also, remember to try this mixture in tacos; it will change your life.

forty cloves of garlic chicken

I know this sounds excessive and I know that you think I'm ridiculous—but neither of those things is true. The beauty of this recipe is in the simplicity and true love of the garlic flavor. It takes the basic concept of garlic confit, which is just garlic that you can spread on bread, crackers, toast or your tongue and be happy. This chicken takes minimal effort but tastes like you're sitting under the Eiffel Tower at a 5-star French restaurant and all you need to complete your night is a violinist at your table serenading you while you eat dinner. Okay, back to reality: Make this chicken. The secret to making this is a skillet or a pan that is stove top– and oven-safe.

Makes 4–6 Servings

8 bone-in, skin-on chicken thighs

½ cup (120 ml) olive oil, divided

3 tbsp (54 g) salt

3 tbsp (18 g) pepper

3 tbsp (21 g) paprika

2 tbsp (24 g) Cajun seasoning

6 thyme sprigs

40 cloves peeled garlic, whole

Preheat your oven to 350°F (176°C).

Season the chicken with 2 tablespoons (30 ml) of oil and salt, pepper, paprika and Cajun seasoning. Rub the spices all over the chicken thighs so they are evenly seasoned all over.

In an oven-safe skillet over medium heat, cook the chicken until browned for about 5 to 7 minutes on each side. You're just looking to get color on all sides of the chicken; it doesn't have to be fully cooked as we are going to bake it through.

Remove from the heat and add 6 tablespoons (90 ml) olive oil, thyme sprigs and garlic cloves. Cover the skillet and bake for 1 hour.

Make sure to have enough toasted bread to spread the garlic cloves on. Any leftover garlic cloves can be put into a jar and stored in the fridge to be used later. They will keep about 2 to 3 weeks.

crab-stuffed cheddar biscuits

When I was a kid, I remember that going to Red Lobster was a massive deal. You thought you were someone super important and fancy when you heard you were going to Red Lobster. The one thing you don't forget is the biscuits. Those cheddar biscuits were and are what dreams are made of. I will go on record and say that when I was pregnant with my daughter, one of my biggest cravings were those biscuits. I will neither confirm nor deny that I ate six in one sitting. Now if you've ever had those biscuits, imagine filling them with seasoned crab. Yes, this is happiness.

Makes 4–6 Servings

8 oz (226 g) shredded Mexican cheese blend

2 (16-oz [454-g]) tubes of Grands! Southern Homestyle Original Biscuits

16 oz (454 g) lump crab meat

3 tbsp (23 g) Old Bay seasoning

½ cup (114 g) butter

1 tbsp (8 g) garlic powder

½ tsp parsley flakes

Preheat the oven to 350°F (176°C).

Prepare a 12-count muffin tin with cupcake liners. Sprinkle about a tablespoon (7 g) of the shredded Mexican cheese blend into each liner.

Open the cans of biscuits and split each biscuit horizontally down the middle. Press one half into the cheese-lined tins, making sure to keep some dough hanging over the tin for crimping later. Set aside the tops of each biscuit.

In a bowl, mix together the crab and Old Bay seasoning, and fill each muffin cavity with about 2 tablespoons of the crab mix. Place a thin slice of butter on top of the crab mix in each cavity. Cover each biscuit with its top half. Crimp the sides of the biscuits, making sure to seal all the crab mixture into each biscuit. Make a small hole with your knife in the top of each of the biscuits.

In a bowl, melt the butter and add the garlic powder and parsley flakes. Brush the top of each biscuit with this garlic butter and bake in the oven for 13 to 15 minutes or until golden brown. Sprinkle the tops with the rest of the shredded cheese and bake again for 2 to 3 minutes or until the cheese is melted.

Remove from the oven and enjoy having your dreams come true.

chicken potato pesto bake

When I originally made this recipe, I was cleaning out my fridge and I was told there was so much that was being wasted. Not for long, buddy! The hardest part of this recipe is the potato chopping. I do make it easy in that I only cut each potato into quarters—that's just two slices per potato. Also, you are welcome to make your own pesto, but honestly my local grocer has an amazing recipe and makes it fresh every day—I'll take the help wherever I can get it. Buying that pesto premade means that I don't have to take out the blender, and even worse, clean the blender. If only I could tell you the amount of times I have cut my fingers on that blade. Anyway, my point is, I buy my pesto, but you can definitely make your own if you like.

Makes 4–6 Servings

2 lb (907 g) red potatoes, quartered

2 cups (182 g) broccoli florets

¼ cup (60 ml) olive oil

1 tsp salt

½ tsp pepper

½ tsp garlic powder

½ tsp paprika

7 oz (198 g) pesto

1 cup (240 ml) sour cream

1 rotisserie chicken, shredded

1 cup (112 g) bacon crumbles

2 cups (226 g) shredded cheddar cheese

Preheat the oven to 350°F (176°C).

In a 3-quart (2.8-L) oven-safe baking dish, combine the cut potatoes, broccoli florets, olive oil, salt, pepper, garlic powder and paprika. Make sure that all the seasonings are all over the potatoes and broccoli.

In a separate bowl, combine the pesto, sour cream, rotisserie chicken and bacon crumbles and mix together. Place this mixture on top of the veggies.

Bake covered (I use foil) for 45 minutes. Remove the cover, add shredded cheddar cheese on top, and bake for another 10 to 15 minutes or until the cheese is melted and brown.

creamy tomato soup

Why did I always think that tomato soup was so complicated to make? It's not. It really is not. The funny part is, if you know me, you know that I hate tomatoes. But give me a bowl of tomato soup and you've won my heart. I know it's weird. It just is what it is. When I realized that you can make tomato soup that tastes amazing more easily than you can open and heat up the ones that come in a box, my life changed. The only real thing you need is a blender.

Makes 4–6 Servings

6 Roma tomatoes, halved

I red bell pepper, chopped

8–10 cloves garlic

I yellow onion, quartered

½ cup (120 ml) olive oil

2 tbsp (36 g) salt

I tbsp (6 g) pepper

2–3 sprigs of thyme

I tbsp (4 g) Italian seasoning

10–12 basil leaves

I cup (240 ml) vegetable stock

½ cup (120 ml) heavy cream

Preheat your oven to 400°F (205°C).

To an oven-safe dish, add the tomatoes, red bell pepper, garlic cloves, onion, olive oil, salt, pepper, thyme and Italian seasoning and bake for 45 minutes.

Once the tomatoes come out of the oven, add everything to a blender with the basil leaves, vegetable stock and heavy cream and blend till smooth.

I don't think anything goes better with tomato soup than a grilled cheese sandwich. You got this!

spaghetti bake

No matter how many fancy restaurants I've been to or how many different types of food I can eat, I always come back to spaghetti. Anyone can boil noodles and add sauce, but this is different. This is baked cheesy goodness and it just takes spaghetti to another level. I use a really good spaghetti sauce to make sure it tastes like it's been cooked all day. If you don't like ground beef, you can always use ground chicken or even fake ground meat, but make sure you layer everything well before you bake!

Makes 4–6 Servings

16 oz (454 g) spaghetti

2 tbsp (30 ml) olive oil

1 small onion, chopped

1 lb (454 g) ground beef

24 oz (680 g) spaghetti sauce

8 oz (226 g) cream cheese

¼ cup (60 ml) sour cream

1 cup (246 g) ricotta cheese

4 tbsp (57 g) butter

1 cup (113 g) shredded cheddar cheese

Cherry tomatoes, halved, for garnish

Fresh basil for garnish

Preheat your oven to 350°F (176°C).

Cook your spaghetti according to the package directions, making sure that you salt the water. Once cooked, drain and set aside.

Into a skillet over medium heat, add your olive oil and onions and cook until translucent. Add in your ground beef and brown until there is no pink left. Drain the fat and add in your spaghetti sauce.

In a mixing bowl, combine the cream cheese, sour cream and ricotta and mix well.

Slice 4 tablespoons (57 g) of butter thinly and put them at the bottom of a 3-quart (2.8-L) oven-safe baking dish. Add half of the cooked spaghetti noodles in an even layer and add the cream cheese mixture on top. Add the rest of the noodles and then add the meat mixture. Make sure everything is in even layers.

Bake for 30 minutes. Add the grated cheese on top and bake for another 10 to 15 minutes until golden brown. Garnish with cherry tomatoes and basil before serving.

southwest chicken alfredo casserole

I always keep taco seasoning stocked in my house. I use it all the time and it is not just for tacos. There is so much goodness in the mixture, it can really flavor anything. I know this is not conventional or traditional. But it's delicious. If you have a really good recipe for Alfredo, please be my guest and use that as your base. I actually buy the Alfredo sauce for this recipe because you need a good amount of it. I also find that rotini pasta works best for this recipe because it really picks up all of the sauce.

Makes 4–6 Servings

16 oz (454 g) rotini pasta

1 rotisserie chicken, shredded

½ cup (80 g) chopped yellow onions

2 (15-oz [425-g]) jars Alfredo sauce

1½ cups (360 ml) salsa

1 cup (246 g) ricotta cheese

1 oz (28 g) taco seasoning

1½ cups (150 g) grated parmesan cheese

Preheat your oven to 350°F (176°C).

Cook the pasta according to the package directions, making sure to salt the water. Drain the pasta and set aside.

In a mixing bowl, combine the shredded chicken, onion, Alfredo sauce, salsa, ricotta cheese, and taco seasoning. Once combined, add in the cooked pasta, put the mixture into a 3-quart (2.8-L) oven-safe baking dish and top with parmesan cheese.

Cover the baking dish with foil and bake for 45 to 50 minutes.

marry me chicken

This recipe has taken over the internet. I don't think it's for the title, but honestly for the result. Rumor has it that this recipe is named what it is because if you make this for your partner, they will want to marry you. You will be in love not only with this dish at first bite but also with the person who made it. It's that good. There is a reason they say that the way to someone's heart is through their stomach. This chicken is swimming in one of the best cream sauces you will ever have.

Makes 4–6 Servings

2 large boneless skinless chicken breasts

½ cup (63 g) flour

I tsp salt

I tsp pepper

I tsp garlic powder

I tsp paprika

2 tbsp (28 g) butter

2 tbsp (30 ml) olive oil

2 tbsp (17 g) garlic, chopped

I cup (240 ml) chicken broth

I cup (240 ml) heavy cream

I cup (100 g) grated parmesan cheese

½ tsp red pepper flakes

½ tsp oregano

⅓ cup (18 g) chopped sun-dried tomatoes

Fresh basil for garnish

Butterfly the chicken breasts by cutting them horizontally through the middle, making four thinner pieces of chicken. On a plate, combine the flour, salt, pepper, garlic powder and paprika. Coat each piece of chicken with the flour mixture and set aside.

In a skillet over medium heat, warm the butter and olive oil for I minute. Add the chicken and cook 5 minutes on each side. Take out the chicken and set aside on a clean plate.

To the same skillet, add the garlic, chicken broth and heavy cream. Bring to a slow boil and add the parmesan, red pepper flakes, oregano and sun-dried tomatoes. Cook for I to 2 minutes and add back in the chicken. Let simmer for 5 minutes and top with basil for garnish.

Now feed this to the one you love and be ready to get married. Lol.

stove top chicken

As an online food creator, I always get asked, "What is your favorite food?" My answer is always the same. Food in general is my favorite. Yet there is a definitive answer and my family knows what it is. Thanksgiving food is my favorite food. Thanksgiving is my time to shine and there's something about turkey and stuffing and green beans and gravy and corn that just makes me happy. This recipe doesn't have turkey; it has chicken because I'm not about to make a whole turkey for a weeknight dinner. Also, every year for Thanksgiving there will be stove top stuffing on my table. I don't care what you say or how much you try to change my mind; it will forever be stove top. Pro tip for this recipe: You can definitely warm up some gravy to top each serving. You're welcome.

Makes 4–6 Servings

1⅔ cups (400 ml) hot water

1 (6-oz [170-g]) box stove-top chicken stuffing

2 tbsp (28 g) butter

2 cups (480 g) chopped green beans

1 tsp salt

1 tsp pepper

1 rotisserie chicken, shredded

⅓ cup (80 ml) milk

1 (10.5-oz [297-g]) can cream of chicken soup

¼ cup (28 g) shredded cheddar cheese

Preheat your oven to 350°F (176°C).

In a bowl, mix together the hot water and stove top stuffing mix and set aside while you assemble everything else.

Into a skillet over medium heat, add the butter and green beans. Season with salt and pepper and sauté until softened.

Into a 3-quart (2.8-L) oven-safe baking dish, add the shredded rotisserie chicken. Add in the milk, cream of chicken soup and cheese and mix with the chicken. Layer the green beans on top of the chicken. Layer the stove top stuffing on top of the green beans and bake for 20 minutes until the stuffing is nice and crispy.

It might not be November when you're reading this, but tell me that doesn't taste like Thanksgiving.

honey chicken

This recipe is almost too easy. The key is to use chicken thighs because they are so full of flavor and don't get tough and dry like chicken breasts. The honey in this recipe creates an amazing sticky sauce that is flavorful and satisfying. You can plate this family style over a bed of mashed potatoes, serve on top of rice, or eat it wrapped in a tortilla like a burrito. The possibilities are endless and delicious.

Makes 4–6 Servings

2 tbsp (30 ml) olive oil

2 tbsp (28 g) butter

1 lb (454 g) boneless skinless chicken thighs, cut into bite-size pieces

2 tsp (12 g) salt

1 tsp pepper

1 tsp paprika

3 tbsp (45 ml) honey

4–5 cloves garlic, chopped

2 tbsp (30 ml) soy sauce

2 tbsp (30 ml) apple cider vinegar

Parsley to garnish

To a skillet over medium heat, add the olive oil and butter. Once the butter is melted, add the chicken pieces and season with salt, pepper and paprika. Brown the chicken until fully cooked.

Add the honey, garlic, soy sauce and apple cider vinegar, and cook for 5 to 7 minutes until the chicken is coated fully.

Garnish with parsley and serve over rice or mashed potatoes.

tomato, cheese and chicken one pot pasta

What's better than tomatoes, pasta and cheese that come together in one beautiful pot? If you've ever sliced mozzarella and tomatoes and topped it with fresh basil, balsamic vinegar and salt and pepper, you'll love this dish. If you want to take this recipe to the next level, toast panko breadcrumbs in butter and top the pasta with them as a final step.

Makes 4–6 Servings

2 tbsp (30 ml) olive oil

1 lb (454 g) chicken breast

2 tbsp (14 g) paprika, divided

2 tbsp (9 g) dried basil, divided

2 tbsp (6 g) dried oregano, divided

2 tbsp (36 g) salt, divided

2 tbsp (13 g) pepper, divided

1 yellow onion, chopped

3–4 cloves garlic, chopped

4 cups (960 ml) chicken stock

2 cups (298 g) cherry tomatoes, halved

8 oz (226 g) bowtie pasta

1 cup (226 g) mini mozzarella balls

Balsamic glaze for garnish

Chopped fresh basil for garnish

Into a stock pot over medium heat, add the olive oil. Cut your chicken into bite-sized pieces and add to the stock pot. Add 1 tablespoon (7 g) paprika, 1 tablespoon (5 g) basil, 1 tablespoon (3 g) oregano, 1 tablespoon (18 g) salt and 1 tablespoon (6 g) pepper. Sauté the chicken until it is cooked through. Transfer the cooked chicken to a bowl and set aside.

In the same pot, over medium heat, add the chopped onion and garlic and cook for 4 to 5 minutes until there is a light golden color on the onions. Add the chicken stock, cherry tomatoes, 1 tablespoon (7 g) paprika, 1 tablespoon (5 g) basil, 1 tablespoon (3 g) oregano, 1 tablespoon (18 g) salt and 1 tablespoon (6 g) pepper. Mix and cover. Bring to a boil.

Once the stock is boiling, add in the dried pasta and stir. Let boil uncovered until the chicken stock has been absorbed into the pasta. Add back in the chicken and the mini mozzarella balls. Toss.

Put the pasta in a serving bowl and swirl the balsamic glaze over the pasta. Add fresh chopped basil to garnish.

cheesy french onion pork chops

Pork chops are one of those things that I don't usually reach for. I think they can be dry and don't always hit the spot. On the other hand, a bowl of French onion soup on a menu is something that I will always order, without a doubt. This recipe is the perfect way to make moist and flavorful pork chops that combine the best of both those worlds. I like the depth of flavor that you get from the condensed soup in this recipe; it's that "cooked all day" flavor. If you don't like pork or choose not to eat pork, you can always substitute with chicken breast, but make sure you slice them very thinly to cook them all the way through.

Makes 4–6 Servings

2 lb (907 g) pork chops, sliced thin

12 oz (360 ml) sour cream

1 (10-oz [283-g]) can French onion condensed soup

2 cups (226 g) shredded mozzarella cheese

2 cups (112 g) crispy French onions

1 tbsp (4 g) Italian seasoning

Preheat the oven to 350°F (176°C).

In the bottom of a 3-quart (2.8-L) oven-safe dish, place the raw pork chops in an even layer, making sure to not overlap them on top of each other.

In a mixing bowl, stir together the sour cream and French onion soup and top the pork chops with this mix. Make sure to cover all of the pork chops. Top the dip with an even layer of mozzarella cheese.

Top the cheese mix with the French onions and season with the Italian seasoning.

Cover the dish with foil and bake for 50 minutes. Remove the foil, then broil the dish on low for 1 to 2 minutes to get a golden brown color on top.

bacon chicken ranch pasta

Yes, this is a cold pasta. Yes, it comes together very quickly. Yes, you will have to fight off the need to eat the whole bowl. The only hard part of this recipe is boiling the pasta. Besides that, this is an exercise in chopping. Chop everything real good. The ranch flavor is so refreshing and full of comforting flavor that you just can't get enough.

Makes 4–6 Servings

16 oz (454 g) rotini pasta

1 cup (240 ml) sour cream

1 cup (240 ml) mayo

½ cup (120 ml) milk

2 oz (57 g) dry ranch seasoning

¼ cup (12 g) chopped green onions

½ tsp salt

½ tsp pepper

1 rotisserie chicken, shredded

1 cup (112 g) bacon crumbles

1 cup (154 g) canned corn

½ cup (80 g) chopped red onions

½ cup (75 g) chopped red bell pepper

½ cup (75 g) chopped yellow bell pepper

½ cup (46 g) chopped cooked broccoli

In a pot, cook your pasta al dente following the package directions, making sure to salt the water. Once cooked, drain the pasta and set aside to cool.

To a mixing bowl, add the sour cream, mayo, milk, ranch seasoning, green onions, salt and pepper. Mix this very well, making sure everything is incorporated. Add the cold pasta, chicken, bacon, corn, red onions, red bell pepper, yellow bell pepper and broccoli.

Toss. Get the dressing all over everything and that's it. Enjoy cold.

when . . .
you want it to
look like it took
a lot of effort

Do you ever think of certain meals as difficult or fancy? Honestly, that's only because of the way they are presented to us in restaurants. Also, some actually complicated dishes can be broken down by taste concepts and made to look or taste the same. Just think of your favorite restaurant's food, but made super easy and super fast all in the comfort of your own home, and if you want—even in your PJs.

chicken pot pie casserole

Chicken pot pie may be one of my favorite comfort foods of all time. This deconstructed pie can feed the whole family very quickly and gives you the same comfy feeling as those individual pies that you remember. I suggest using shredded rotisserie chicken; it helps with the flavor and makes it taste like it has been cooking all day. You can even make the filling in large batches and freeze it in individual packets; that way you can defrost and microwave what you need and add on a biscuit.

Makes 4–6 Servings

2 (16-oz [454-g]) tubes of Grands! Flaky Layers Original Biscuits

I rotisserie chicken, shredded

12 oz (340 g) frozen mixed vegetables

2 (10-oz [283-g]) cans cream of chicken soup

1 tbsp (18 g) salt

1 tbsp (6 g) pepper

1 tbsp (7 g) onion powder

1 tbsp (8 g) garlic powder

½ tsp dried parsley

3 tbsp (36 g) Cajun seasoning

Preheat your oven to 350°F (176°C).

Quarter each biscuit. I used to put these directly onto the top of the casserole, but sometimes the middle ones wouldn't cook all the way. For this reason, I now put all the cut-up biscuits on a cookie sheet next to the casserole and then add them on top after they are fully cooked.

In an oven-safe 3-quart (2.8-L) baking dish, mix the shredded chicken, frozen mixed vegetables, soup, salt, pepper, onion powder, garlic powder, dried parsley and Cajun seasoning. Put the casserole and the biscuits in the oven. After about 15 minutes, flip the biscuit pieces. Bake for 15 more minutes.

You can choose to either add all of the biscuit pieces on top of the casserole, or put the chicken mix into bowls and let everyone add biscuit pieces to their own bowl. I will let you in on a secret—our family chooses option two these days.

southwest eggrolls

We have all been to a restaurant that makes these. It's funny to me because they're always categorized as appetizers, but let me tell you I will always order them as my dinner. I love love love Southwest Eggrolls. They are a whole meal that I don't have to do anything special with and can dip into my favorite ranch dressing. The best part is they are super easy to make. The only part of this recipe that seems kind of daunting is the frying, but I have used the air fryer and that works beautifully. Also, when you make this recipe you can always double it and freeze the eggrolls; they make perfect afternoon or after-school snacks.

Makes 4–6 Servings

10 oz (283 g) frozen spinach

8 oz (226 g) cream cheese, room temperature

8 oz (226 g) shredded Mexican cheese

2 cups (140 g) shredded rotisserie chicken

1 cup (150 g) red bell pepper, finely chopped

1 cup (50 g) chopped green onions

1 oz (28 g) fajita seasoning

Neutral oil for frying

12 large wonton wrappers

1 tbsp (18 g) coarse salt

Put the spinach in the microwave for 4 to 5 minutes to thaw. Remove the water that is released from the spinach and put the spinach into a bowl. Add in the cream cheese, Mexican cheese, shredded rotisserie chicken, chopped red bell pepper, green onions and fajita seasoning. Make sure to mix this well so that all the seasoning and cheese is equally distributed.

In a pot suitable for frying, heat the neutral oil over medium heat and prepare a paper napkin–lined plate where you will place the wontons after frying.

Lay one wonton wrapper on a cutting board and scoop 3 tablespoons (45 g) of the mixture onto the wonton wrapper. Fold the bottom part over the mixture first, then each side into the middle and then roll the rest of the wonton upward. Right at the end of the roll, you want to put just a little bit of water to hold the egg roll closed. Don't put too much water as you are going to fry the eggroll and the water will make the oil splatter. Repeat with the other 11 wonton wrappers.

Fry the eggrolls to golden brown. Once the eggrolls come out of the oil, sprinkle some coarse salt on top. I like to dip these in a ranch dressing for that perfect restaurant-style presentation.

butter chicken

I am Punjabi; that means my culture and ancestry share an origin with this Butter Chicken. Right off the bat, this is not an authentic Indian recipe. This is a recipe that I made to get to as close to the real stuff that takes forever to make the right way. I make it during the week for my kids, who love butter chicken, and also for people who are coming over last minute and want Indian food. This recipe for sure hits the spot. Original butter chicken actually uses tandoori chicken that was made especially for that meal or, more often than not, tandoori chicken that was left over from another meal. My hack for this flavor—you guessed it—is shredded rotisserie chicken. It has flavor and is soft and cooked in a pit like real tandoori chicken is. Trust me, this hacked butter chicken recipe can go up against any Indian takeout.

Makes 4–6 Servings

1 jalapeño

8 tbsp (114 g) butter

1 yellow onion, grated

4–5 cloves garlic

2 tsp (10 g) minced ginger

28 oz (840 ml) tomato puree

2 tsp (12 g) salt

½ tsp sugar

2 tbsp (12 g) cumin

1 tsp chili powder

3 tbsp (19 g) curry powder

2 cups (480 ml) heavy cream

1 lb (454 g) shredded rotisserie chicken

½ cup (8 g) chopped cilantro

Prep the jalapeño. Depending on the level of spice you can handle, you can choose to leave the seeds in if you like it with a little heat, or take them out if you're a spice chicken like me. You can either finely chop it or cut it lengthwise so that you can remove it when the dish is finished. That way, the flavor is there but nobody has to bite down on it.

Into a skillet over medium heat, add the butter and onion and brown. Add in the garlic, ginger and jalapeño. Cook for 1 to 2 minutes.

Add in the tomato puree and season with salt, sugar, cumin, chili powder and curry powder. Mix and cook for 2 to 3 minutes to cook all the spices. Add in your heavy cream. Mix to combine and taste to adjust for salt.

Add the shredded rotisserie chicken to the sauce and mix to coat. Top with the cilantro and your kitchen is no less than an Indian takeout spot. Pour this over some basmati rice or dip in with toasted naan bread for the perfect meal.

basil chicken potato hash

This recipe comes to you from a very special place in my heart. The part that could sit in front of the TV and eat a whole pan of this hash. There is something about chicken and potatoes cooked to crispy perfection, topped with melty beautiful cheese; I'm drooling as I write this. I do prefer to make sure I have fresh basil for this meal. The dried stuff just doesn't do it. This dish comes together all in one pan and just has to be cooked in layers and steps to get everything crispy and yummy.

Makes 4–6 Servings

4 tbsp (60 ml) olive oil

4 tbsp (56 g) butter

2 lb (907 g) Idaho potatoes, peeled and finely diced

1 tsp salt

1 tsp pepper

1 red onion, finely diced

1 red bell pepper, finely diced

4–5 cloves garlic, minced

To a skillet over medium heat, add the olive oil and butter. When the butter is melted, add in the diced potatoes and season them with salt and pepper. Make sure to not move them too much so that they can get the perfect brown crispy crust on them. Cook for about 8 to 10 minutes or until the potatoes are soft when tested with a fork and cooked through.

Add the onions, bell peppers and garlic. Cook for 3 to 5 minutes or until the onions and bell peppers both are tender.

2 tbsp (32 g) tomato paste

2 tsp (5 g) paprika

¼ cup (60 ml) hot water

1 rotisserie chicken, shredded

8 oz (226 g) shredded cheddar cheese

4 green onions, chopped

¼ cup (4 g) chopped cilantro

10 basil leaves

Add in the tomato paste, paprika and hot water. Stir and add the shredded rotisserie chicken. Fold everything together so everything is fully incorporated into the tomato paste. Turn off the heat and top with the shredded cheddar cheese, green onions, cilantro and basil.

shrimp and chicken summer rolls with peanut sauce

Imagine you live in Florida and during the summer it is about 102 degrees on a good day. Also, imagine that you have three kids that just want to play outside, no matter the temperature. What is something that I can feed these littles that is not hot or a dish they truly have to sit down for, and has protein and veggies that they love? Shrimp and Chicken Summer Rolls have entered the chat. These are so good and so light but full of great nutrients and I love that they are cold and handheld. You can again add any proteins you like or no proteins at all and just make them veggie filled; the possibilities are endless.

Makes 4–6 Servings

12 rice paper wrappers

1 flat plate of cold water

1 English cucumber, sliced

1 cup (50 g) green onions, sliced

1 head of shredded lettuce

1 cup (16 g) chopped cilantro

1 rotisserie chicken, shredded

1 lb (454 g) cooked shrimp, halved horizontally

The only thing about this recipe is that you need to work one roll at a time. Dip the rice paper wrapper in the plate of cold water on both sides and lay it on a clean cutting board. Add some cucumbers, green onions, shredded lettuce and cilantro.

Fold over the right side then the left side. Take the bottom and roll over all the veggies but stop once the veggies are covered. This little pocket is where you are going to put the protein or proteins of choice. I like to add a layer of shredded chicken and three of the halved shrimps for my rolls. Then, continue rolling the rice paper and it will stick to itself at the end.

For the Sauce

3 tbsp (48 g) peanut butter

1 tsp soy sauce

1 tsp sesame oil

1 tsp sriracha

1 tsp sesame seeds

To make the sauce, mix the peanut butter, soy sauce, sesame oil and sriracha in a bowl. Top with sesame seeds, and you're ready to dip your summer rolls into the perfect umami sauce.

taco
pasta salad

There's something to say about a dish where you can use Doritos as croutons. This is something I make in big batches for dinner, but I also make it if I have to take something to a potluck, a picnic or someone I love so that they don't have to cook that night. Imagine all the goodness of a taco but with pasta and in a plate. Yes, all your dreams can come true with this phenomenal meal.

Makes 4–6 Servings

16 oz (454 g) bowtie pasta

2 tbsp (30 ml) olive oil

1 small onion, chopped

1 tsp salt

1 lb (454 g) ground beef

1 (1-oz [28-g]) packet taco seasoning mix

¾ cup (180 ml) water

8 oz (226 g) shredded cheddar cheese

2 cups (298 g) grape tomatoes

½ cup (8 g) cilantro

1 red bell pepper

½ cup (90 g) black olives

2 cups (126 g) crushed Doritos®

3 avocados

1 cup (240 ml) sour cream

Fill a pot with salted water and cook the pasta al dente according to the box directions. Once the pasta is cooked, drain, run under cold water and set aside.

Into a skillet over medium heat, add the olive oil and onions, season with salt and cook until translucent. Add the ground beef and cook until there is no pink left in the meat. Don't drain the fat. Add the taco seasoning and the water and let the meat soak in all the water.

In a serving bowl, combine the cold noodles, cooked beef, shredded cheese, grape tomatoes, cilantro, bell pepper and black olives. Mix to create the base of everyone's taco salad.

Top with crushed Doritos, avocado and sour cream as needed on each person's plate.

honey mustard salmon

This is not your average salmon. There is texture, there is flavor, there is minimal effort and because it's baked, there is no guilt when you go back for more. When you make this, be prepared to have everyone ask you for the recipe. I actually thought of keeping this recipe to myself because of how many people wanted it, but I'm a lover not a gatekeeper. I had this salmon at a restaurant and liked it so much that I had to come home and re-create it. Once you make this, you too can charge your guests (or kids) $35 a plate.

Makes 4–6 Servings

Nonstick cooking spray

2–2.5 lb (907–1133 g) salmon

½ cup (114 g) salted butter, room temperature

2 tbsp (30 ml) whole grain mustard

1 tbsp (15 ml) honey

1 tsp ground paprika

½ tsp celery seeds

1 tsp garlic powder

1 tbsp (3 g) fresh dill, chopped

Preheat the oven to 350°F (176°C).

Prepare an oven-safe baking tray with nonstick cooking spray and place your salmon in there skin side down. Pat the top of the salmon dry with a paper towel, going over them twice to make sure there is no moisture left or else the seasoning will slip off.

In a bowl, combine the butter, mustard, honey, paprika, celery seeds and garlic powder. Mix until everything is incorporated. Congratulations, you are fancy—this mixture is called compound butter. Spread the butter on top of the salmon in an even layer, covering all of the fish. Bake the salmon for 17 minutes.

After baking, broil on low for 2 minutes. This gives it a beautiful color on top (like a restaurant, wink, wink). Remove the salmon from the oven and top with fresh dill. You can serve the salmon with fresh veggies or on a bed of rice, or both!

avocado chicken salad

When I tell you I never liked chicken salad or ever felt the need to eat cold chicken, it is the truth. That all changed with this recipe. Not only do I eat this, I crave it. The key is to use shredded rotisserie chicken. Rotisserie chicken packs in so much flavor and is so tender, it truly will make anyone a chicken salad believer—including me. It also is a huge time saver and a key for easy and fast meals.

Makes 4–6 Servings

1 lb (454 g) rotisserie chicken

2 avocados, diced, divided

⅔ cup (160 ml) mayo

10–12 drops of your favorite hot sauce

½ tsp salt

¼ tsp pepper

1 tsp celery seeds

1 cup (56 g) crispy French onions

½ cup (8 g) chopped cilantro

This recipe is so simple and so fulfilling. The hardest part is shredding the chicken. Make sure to get it into small pieces; you can leave the skin on or take it off—it's your choice. I like it on because it adds flavor.

Add the shredded chicken to a bowl and add one of the diced avocados, mayo, hot sauce, salt, pepper and celery seeds. Mix and mash these together to form your base.

Add the other diced avocado, keeping it in bigger chunks to add to the texture of the chicken salad. Add the fried onions and the cilantro.

TA-DA! You're done, and ready to eat. I like to scoop this chicken salad onto a leaf of romaine lettuce, but my husband likes to eat his on toasted bread and add other sandwich toppings (tomato, onions and cheese). Whichever way you decide to eat it, I can promise you this will be the chicken salad that even non-chicken-salad eaters will crave.

sun-dried tomato spinach fettuccine

Fun fact about me: I hate tomatoes. Like despise them. I will pick any stray raw tomato out of anything that I eat. Yes, I am 40 years old and this is my life. On the other end of that spectrum, I don't care what anyone says: I love sun-dried tomatoes. I will actually ask for extra if they are in something that I order. Again, yes this is my life and these are things I do. This dish has the best sun-dried tomato flavor. Obsessed.

Makes 4–6 Servings

1 lb (454 g) fettuccine pasta

4 tbsp (60 ml) olive oil

4–5 cloves garlic, minced

½ cup (27 g) sun-dried tomatoes, chopped

8 oz (226 g) fresh baby spinach

1 (14.5-oz [410-g]) can diced tomatoes

3 tbsp (48 g) tomato paste

1½ cups (360 ml) heavy cream

½ cup (120 ml) sour cream

1 tsp crushed red pepper flakes, optional

1 tsp salt

1 tsp pepper

2 tbsp (7 g) Italian seasoning

1 cup (100 g) grated parmesan cheese

Cook the fettuccine pasta according to the box directions and set aside. Make sure to salt your water when you make your pasta so that the noodles are not bland when you add them to the sauce.

Into a skillet over medium heat, add the olive oil and warm up your garlic. Don't get it too hot or let it burn. As soon as it's warm, add in the sun-dried tomatoes, fresh spinach and diced tomatoes. Cook the tomatoes down and mash them a bit. After cooking for 3 to 5 minutes, add in the tomato paste and mix.

Add the heavy cream, sour cream and crushed red pepper flakes if using and stir to combine. Let this simmer and get all bubbly. Add the salt, pepper, Italian seasoning and parmesan to finish off the sauce.

Toss in the cooked fettuccine and let the sauce sit for a few minutes before serving. Always feel free to add parmesan cheese on top of each portion. It's only polite.

crab rangoon eggrolls

Crab rangoons may be the most satisfying food you can get from a Chinese restaurant: Crispy egg roll crust filled with creamy, crabby deliciousness. But there's something about the size of these little treats that's never enough. Hence, the crab rangoon eggroll was born. These longer and more fun-filled treats are so good because they are a fulfilling meal. My favorite sauce for these treats is Mae Ploy® sauce from my local Asian market. The sweet, spicy sauce is what makes these rangoons taste exactly like a Chinese-restaurant treat.

Makes 4–6 Servings

8 oz (226 g) cream cheese, room temperature

8 oz (226 g) imitation crab, finely chopped

4 green onions, chopped

2 tbsp (30 ml) sesame oil

2 tbsp (30 ml) soy sauce

1 tbsp (15 ml) garlic chili oil

Neutral oil for frying

20 wonton wrappers

2 tbsp (36 g) coarse salt

In a bowl, combine the cream cheese, crab, green onions, sesame oil, soy sauce and garlic chili oil. Mix well and set aside.

In a large deep pot suitable for frying, warm the frying oil over medium heat. Prepare a plate lined with paper towels.

Scoop 2 tablespoons (30 g) of the mixture into the middle of a wonton wrapper and roll it like a burrito. By this I mean fold the sides in first and then roll from the bottom up. Repeat with the other 19 wrappers.

Fry the wontons 2 to 3 at a time so as not to cool down the oil. Remove from the oil when the wontons are golden brown. Place on the prepared plate and top with a little coarse salt.

crab sushi balls

I truly wish I was the type of person who could get it together enough to make beautiful rolls of sushi. I am not that person. I am the type of person who can figure out the fastest way to feed not only myself but also everyone around me. These crab rice balls are like if a sushi roll and a meatball had a baby. You can always switch out the crab for either cooked salmon or even chopped uncooked shrimp, but the crab is the real win for me. I use real lump crab meat for this recipe, but if for some reason you can't find real crab, you can always use imitation crab; just make sure to chop it really finely. I also use a mini ice cream scoop to get the same amount for each ball.

Makes 4–6 Servings

1 (0.35-oz [9-g]) package seaweed sheets

2 cups (372 g) cooked jasmine rice

8 oz (226 g) lump crab meat

4 green onions, chopped

½ cup (120 ml) kewpie mayo

¼ cup (60 ml) sriracha

2 tbsp (14 g) furikake seasoning

2 tbsp (30 ml) soy sauce

In a food processor, blend all the seaweed sheets until they are shredded and set aside.

In a bowl, mix the rice, crab, green onions, mayo, sriracha, furikake seasoning and soy sauce. Use a mini ice cream scoop to scoop equal portions of the mixture into your hand and roll each into a ball. Repeat until all of the mixture has been used.

Place the rolled balls into the fridge for 3 to 5 minutes so that the rice sets a bit. Then, roll each ball in the shredded seaweed sheets, making sure each ball is coated with the seaweed all the way around.

acknowledgments

To my husband: When I lost myself as a mother of three, you encouraged me to do things that made me happy. You were never one to edit me, in any form, so you've always been my loudest cheerleader. We've been married for 14 years; you have seen a lot of ups and more importantly lots of downs. No matter how bad our day was, you always kept me and our kids as priority number one. Thank you, Ranjit, for letting me fly.

I want to thank one of the most important people in my life, A. Singh. You have made me realize I can achieve more than I ever thought I could. You make me happy every day. I love you.

I want to take this time to thank my publisher. Thank you so much for believing in me and in this vision. I cannot tell you how much it means to me that you gave me creative freedom and backed me in every way. To my editor, thank you for seeing the light at the end of the tunnel and making sure I got there with everything that I wanted. You truly made all this happen.

Thank you to my amazing photographer; you captured every recipe the way I think of it in my head. Your talent is unparalleled.

Thank you Tamsin Wright for shooting the cover of this book. Your talent for catching a person's vision and personality is amazing. Our 12-year-old selves would be so proud of us today.

To all my fans and followers on all my social media channels: None of this would be possible without you. Thank you for letting me into your lives and even more importantly—thank you for coming into mine.

about the author

Hello! My name is Sophia and I am a native Floridian, born in Orlando and raised in Melbourne. I am a very blessed wife and mom of three beautiful children. My passion has always been in the kitchen. My mom taught me how to make rice when I was about 10 and since then I have been obsessed with creating. I still remember taking Home Economics in high school and coming home so excited to make the things I learned. I was very thankful that I was encouraged to do everything that made me happy. Over the years, baking really became a passion of mine, so much so that when I got married, I moved to London (where my husband is from) and opened a cake shop. Even though it was short-lived, creating in that shop was a true passion and made me happy when I was very homesick. When my first child came along, I realized I didn't always have the time or energy for cooking and baking in the traditional sense. Like most new moms, I got lost in being a mom. Over the next few years, we added two more beautiful babies to our family, and I began to feel like all I was was a mom. I had no time for the things I loved and when I did have time—I needed sleep. Insert cooking hacks and tips here! I didn't always need hours to cook and that's what I learned really fast. A few years ago when the pandemic changed everyone's world, I downloaded this little app called TikTok. TikTok gave me life again. It gave me time for me and made me remember that yes, I was a mother, but I was also a person. A fully functioning human person, with thoughts and recipes that could help others. Thus, A Quick Spoonful was born. This journey has been the best of my life and has made so many amazing dreams of mine, which I thought were long gone, a reality. I appreciate all of you who have supported me along the way. You have given this mom the ability to dream again. This book is a compilation of all my go-to dinners that I have made over the past 20 years, and some new ones that are our family's new favorites.

index